BeeCause You

Loved Me

The true story of how a simple bee sting crippled a man, upended family, shattered dreams, and taught everyone how true love can prevail.

Monique L. Muñoz

Bellevue, Washington, USA

BeeCause You Loved Me

Author: Monique L. Muñoz
Published by: Monique L. Muñoz
BELLEVUE, WA 98006

Book Cover Design: Monique L. Muñoz

ISBN – 1449589944

Copyright © 2009-2013
Second Edition
Published in the United States of America

For more information about this book and patient and family rights, please visit: www.beecauseyoulovedme.com

BeeCause You Loved Me

Disclaimer

This book is a memoir, an account of how the impact of a simple bee sting affected a family. It was written by Monique L. Muñoz, Rene A. Muñoz's wife.

All comments and reflections in this memoir are from the perspective of the author only.

Every effort has been made to make this book as complete and accurate as possible.

However, there *may be mistakes*, both typographical and in content. Therefore, this text should be considered as general information regarding the journey the author shared with her husband and family.

The purpose of this book is to educate and entertain. The author and her publishing representative shall have neither liability nor responsibility to any person or entity with respect to any loss or damage caused, or alleged to have been caused, directly or indirectly, by the information contained in this book.

If you do not wish to be bound by the above, you may return this book to the publisher for a full refund.

BeeCause You Loved Me

Acknowledgments

First, to the One who holds the world in the palms of His hands who has held me through thick and thin, and without whose mercy and unending grace I would be but a pitiful, whimpering puddle on the floor, curled up in the fetal position and asking for "my blankie." Your grace knows no end, and your mercies ARE new every morning. Thank you, God, for being my Lord and Savior, and my friend.

To Rene, the man who changed my life forever by the simple yet profound act of loving me so much, and who gave me the gift of me. **You will always have a special place in my heart. I am in part who I am today <u>because you loved me</u>**.

To my children, Tyeshia and Joshua, whose love, strength, insight, wisdom, and continued selflessness will forever continue to amaze, inspire, and humble me. Thank you for being such incredible young adults and amazing people. I am honored to be your mother!

To my mother, Freddie, who believed in me when I did not have the strength to believe in myself. Thank you for your unending wisdom and love, for your constant prayers and intercession, and for never giving up on me.

To my "heart friends": Pastors Bob and Mary Ellen, Charity, Jen, Michelle (Rashid!), Jeff H., Rondo, Toni, Michael, Chris H., Shanda, Darcey, Eve, and Vance. You have been there for me during the ups and downs of my life, have literally walked me through the "valley of the shadow of death," have seen me at my best as well as my worst, and have loved me through it all. I am truly a blessed woman, and I am honored to have each one of you in my life.

To every doctor, nurse, and aide—especially "Dr. Mo,"Hagman, Nurse Eric, and my University of Washington Medical Center "family"—thank you for all your medical expertise, love, care, and compassion!

And to every friend, co-worker, or neighbor who provided truly caring and compassionate assistance to either Rene or myself, thank you for taking care of us both physically and emotionally.

BeeCause You Loved Me

BeeCause You Loved Me

Contents

*Bee*Cause You Loved Me

My mind tells me to give up,

but my heart won't let me.

—Anonymous

1

"Me"

I used to think of myself as a sensible and analytical woman, grounded in facts, with a love for knowledge, a passion for technology, and a fear and reverence for God. I was not one to believe in maudlin love, "happily ever after," or "soul mates"—that is, until I met the man that shattered my ideals of reality, upended my analytical sensibilities, and changed my life forever. And that was just the beginning.

I am a woman with eight brothers, and as I frequently remind my siblings, I am the only "estrogen-based unit" in the family. My two elder brothers are nine and seven years older than I am, and there is another significant age difference between all my younger brothers and me. The result? I functioned as the eldest child in the home in which I grew up.

I both married and started my professional technology career at a young age. I was married for sixteen years, and was blessed with two wonderful, beautiful, and magnificent children from that union. However, as for the marriage—well, let's just say that it was one of the key reasons I was so cemented in my disbelief of maudlin love. My theory was that the Bible verse "two become one" in reference to marriage meant that half of me had to be cut off, half of my spouse had to be cut off, then our two halves could be put together to make us "one," and that was why marriage was so painful. Yes, I really did believe that!

I surmised that people married, found out their spouse was different from the person they believed him or her to be, found out that they themselves were different than they thought they were, and then both spent the remainder of their lives trying to reconcile the differences.

I believed that the spectrum of happiness associated with those marriages was dependent upon how much you allowed the pain of the "cutting" to affect you. What I did not know then, and have since learned, is that if one party is unwilling or unable to change, grow, and sacrifice for the marriage, the other party inevitably can almost completely cut himself or herself away, leaving only a shell, and begin to disappear as an individual.

What I also know now is that one person cannot fix it all; one person cannot change enough to adapt to an unwilling or absent partner—a marriage takes two. Moreover, once you have been the "cut" one, your love bank ends up with a negative balance, and only a shell of yourself remains—if you are lucky. If not, you are left wondering who you are, what you have become, and how you got there. That is where I found myself, and in the midst of my contemplation, my heart was unexpectedly and inexplicably changed.

2

Friendship

To categorize Rene as charismatic would seem to be a disservice. It may be more accurate to use words like magnetic, enigmatic, charming, and captivating to describe him. His personality was such that people felt comfortable with and drawn to him. One of his most compelling traits was his sincerity and his love for people. No matter where he was—working on a roof, ministering to hundreds, or preparing bowls of salad to hand out to the homeless—he had a natural way of making people feel relaxed and at ease with him and the people around them. Maybe it was those big brown eyes of his with the long eyelashes, or maybe it was the smile he so freely gave to everyone that caused people to be drawn to him, but whatever it was, it was difficult to resist.

Rene and I initially met during a small group home ministry meeting at my mother's house in Sammamish, Washington. He was a minister my mother had met through a distant cousin of mine.

My cousin took my mother to one of Rene's ministry meetings, and afterward, she met Rene and they became friends.

At the time, my mother was running a staffed residential home for emotionally challenged foster children, many of whom had been physically and sexually abused. It was a nonprofit organization—ministry, really—that I had helped my mother start, and as a result, I was the vice president and on the board of directors.

As the staffed residential home was a Christian-based nonprofit agency, Rene eventually became the spiritual oversight for the organization.

Friendship

Now let us fast-forward to Rene and the Saturday night meetings he began holding in my mother's home, which is where our friendship began.

When I first met Rene, I didn't give him a second thought. In fact, other than recognizing his incredible gift in ministry, I did not give him or other men any thought at all. I was in the throes of ending a bad marriage, and men were the last thing on my mind.

I later found out Rene was at the end of a three-year separation from his wife (her choice, not his), which was finalizing into a divorce. I was not in a state of mind to consider *any* man, as men were *not* an option. Period. Remember, my definition of marriage equated to pain!

Rene held meetings at my mother's home that started out with about twenty people attending, and by the time the meetings were in full force, there were over one hundred people attending every other Saturday evening. He would speak, sing, minister, pray, and prophesy to people (give them words of wisdom and encouragement about their lives and situations as God gave him insight) in a way I had never seen or experienced before. The way God used him was absolutely incredible.

Over time, Rene became a very close friend to many of my family. As the meetings grew, so did the complexity of the setup for speaking, singing, worship, and personal ministry. Being the technology and electronics geek of the bunch, I began to find ways to be more efficient for the meetings.

At first, the sound system was set up so that Rene had to hold a handheld tape recorder to record personal ministries for people. Well, imagine him prophesying to sometimes thirty people or more in one night, with him or someone else holding the tape recorder; it became very tiring and inefficient. It took time to put the tape in, remove it, label it, and put another tape in for the next person, all while people were waiting for the ministry and prophesying to continue.

After learning a little more about our sound system's capabilities, I found that by using a couple of special cables I could use one output to play music from a CD

Friendship

player while Rene ministered, and an input to a tape recorder to record the prophecies.

The new setup no longer required Rene, or anyone else that was ministering, to walk around with a tape recorder, and it allowed the worship team to take breaks during the long personal ministry times.

Can you imagine how much time it takes to minister personally to a hundred people? It often took hours because Rene, bless his heart, would pray for and minister to every person that attended the meeting.

As time went on and the ministry grew, we began attending Rene's own church on Sundays.

As more time passed, Rene became so close to all of us that he was seen as an extended family member, celebrating holidays, birthdays, and special occasions with my mother, brothers, family members, and me and my children.

Since both of us were in the midst of ending long, arduous marriages, Rene and I had a lot in common. We often discussed the issues, trials, and tribulations one faces when a long, bad marriage is at its ending point.

My husband had moved out, and Rene had been sleeping on his family room floor for three years, per his wife's demand. He and I were both emotionally exhausted and definitely not looking for love—which for us did not come until much later.

As friends, we began to discover that we shared a lot of the same interests. We shared our love for God and ministry, our work ethic, passion and love for people (although he and I displayed these in different ways), and the fact that we both had spent most of our adult lives taking care of others, especially our spouses and families. We did not realize that we often did this at the expense of taking care of ourselves.

We were both "givers" and were often surrounded by those who were more than willing to take, but unwilling or unable to give of themselves.

We came to realize that living this way caused us both to be emotionally drained and exhausted.

Friendship

Our common interests were expressed; we loved the same kind of music, had very similar tastes in food, and even liked the same types of movies. Both of us loved comedy, thriller, action, martial arts, true story, and romance movies. (Yes, Rene liked chick flicks, but shhh...don't tell anyone!)

I began working more and more with Rene in his ministry, and our friendship grew. Every once in a while, there would be moments where I felt this odd and powerful electricity between the two of us, something I had never felt before in my life; fleeting moments where I wondered if I was imagining things.

One time, when Rene and I were setting up the soundboard for a meeting, his hand barely touched mine and I felt (for lack of a better word) a "surge" go through my body.

I thought I was losing my mind. How could one simple touch startle my system and make my stomach do somersaults? Well, it did, and that wasn't the only one. There were other "moments." Moments in conversation or in simple interactions where it seemed that one second would last a lifetime.

Time moved on; we worked together on ministry things and started a small ministry school, and every once in a while the moments would happen. However, I tried to ignore them because I thought I was just being silly. For heaven's sake, this man was a pastor and had just gone through a horrific divorce from a woman who once had been the love of his life. I believed that it was not even possible that there was something of substance there, not possible at all. See, there I was, being analytical again, which I soon found out does not work very well when it comes to some matters of the heart.

One evening, Rene and I were on the phone and "it" happened—the conversation. You know, the conversation that forever changes the course of your relationship with someone. The conversation I thought would never happen again, because when it comes to understanding love, let's just say that I am a little "challenged."

I had been on the phone with him for a while, discussing various ministry items, organizing calendars, and other general topics when the call took a significant turn. When it did, it went something like this.

Rene said, "So, is it me, or do I sense that there is something between us?"

Literally dumbfounded, I paused, stuttered, and then considered my options. Was he going to tell me that he had feelings for me, or that he sensed something from me and wanted to put an end to any silly ideas I had? More than likely, I figured the latter was probably the case. The option that he was opening a door to something starting between us was, in my analytical assessment, not possible and definitely not probable. I mean, this man was an inexplicably magnificent person, a minister and a man of God. I had never met anyone quite like him, and in my mind, there was no way that he would be interested in me. So, after I caught my breath, my hesitant, gauged, and not-so-eloquent response was something like this.

"Well, I, um, what do you think? I thought maybe, uh...," I stammered.

And then Rene, being the wonderfully sensitive man that he is, interrupted and rescued me. "That is what I thought. You do not have to try to answer. I already know because I feel the same way."

I think at that point, I felt like my heart stopped, leapt, and landed somewhere between my chest and my throat. Then I started crying—sobbing, actually.

I had no idea how much I had held my feelings inside or how much I had denied them. I did not know how much my heart ached to be cared for and loved. It had been so long since I had felt genuine care from someone that my emotions overtook me. My heart had been broken; my ideals shattered. My thoughts of ever having a loving marriage and family were long gone. I was a Christian single mom taking care of my children; a hard-working, successful businessperson. Thinking that I would be navigating life alone, a love relationship had not been in my purview.

Rene listened to me cry on the phone with a release of emotions. He listened, and in the most amazing, caring, soothing voice, he began to talk to me. "I know, I know," he said, "it has been hard for me, too. I did not want to offend you by asking. I was hoping, but I was not sure. If I was wrong, I would have ruined our wonderful friendship, but I realized it was worth it to me to risk it for what I knew would be something even more beautiful."

My heart melted, and I sighed, sniffled, felt a weight lift off my shoulders, and had a sense of peace I had never felt before in my life.

What could I say to that? This man had come to be a dear friend to my children and me. He knew me, understood me, and had seen me at some of the worst times in my life.

Because we were not dating, were not romantically involved, we did not put up facades with each other. We shared some of our deepest thoughts and fears, laughed through our tears, and showed each other our "real" selves. And knowing all these things, something very special was developing between us.

Rene had seen me fall apart while going through my divorce; had seen my financial strains and my struggles in adapting to becoming a single parent. He had seen my ultimate epiphany that my being a single parent was not all that different than when I was married. I had carried 98.5 percent of the weight then. I had worked, paid the bills, set the spiritual and moral standards for our family, taken care of the kids, and managed the household and all that it entailed. It had both disappointed and angered me to realize how alone I had actually been when my now ex-husband had been in the home.

My moment of epiphany, when I realized how alone I had been, was when I was standing in the kitchen one evening several months after my ex-husband had left. I was cooking dinner and realized I was out of a key ingredient I needed for my recipe, and for the first time since he left, I thought, *Boy, I sure wish my ex-husband was here, because if he were, he could go to the store for me.*

Not once had I missed *him.* I had not missed his presence or our talks, because we did not really *talk and share* with each other. He did not share himself with me. I had not missed his advice, because over the years there

Friendship

had been little. I had not missed spending time with him, because that was always strained and lacked the most basic forms of intimacy. I had not missed his compliments, reassurance, or laughter, which were virtually nonexistent as well. I did not miss his financial support because it had been a struggle for him to keep consistent jobs, most of which paid little more than minimum wage.

At that moment in the kitchen, I cried. No, I wept. The tears I shed and emotions I felt were not because my ex-husband wasn't there anymore; they were because I didn't miss him. His presence wasn't missed. I realized then that I had been alone much longer than several months. I had been alone in my marriage for many, many years.

As Rene and I continued our conversation, I knew that he had seen the anger, the disgust, and my sometimes mistrust of people due to all the hurts I had experienced in my life. He had seen me retreat from being an extrovert, staying at home and mending my wounds. He had seen me question myself, my life, my world, even my purpose. For goodness' sake, he had even seen my "ugly" cry. Yet, he said he wanted something more with me, and that "more" could be even more beautiful than our friendship.

He listened to me cry and said, "It's OK. It is all going to be OK. You have had to be strong on your own for way too long. I am here now, and I will be here for you. We are going to try this, and it is going to work because of who we are and how our hearts have already begun binding together."

And so, in that phone call, with one simple yet extremely complex question, our love relationship officially began.

I wonder what would have happened if I had answered his question with no?

3

Falling

I awoke the next morning in a slight fog initially, vaguely remembering the previous night's phone call and wondering if the late-night conversation had been a dream. However, once the fog lifted, I realized that I had subconsciously been hoping for and dreaming of that conversation for a long time. Not specifically with Rene, but what I had hoped would come to pass; that my life would be shared with someone who wanted more, wanted me, and wanted to share his life with me. It was what I had fought and tried so hard to acquire during my previous sixteen years of marriage, but, without a willing partner, was unable to achieve. I realized, as I fully awoke, that the previous night's call could be the beginning of my dreams and hopes taking their first steps to becoming reality.

So, we had had "the conversation." We finally got "it" out in the air. Now what were we going to do?

We talked again, somewhat tentatively at first, both slightly apprehensive that the other would lament the fact that we had admitted our affections to each other. However, very quickly both of us realized that we were relieved and excited about the new path our friendship was taking.

We met later that day, to talk in person. I guess we both needed to look into each other's eyes, more for reassurance of taking this next step than anything else. We sat, talked, and discussed the "pros and cons" of our pursing a romantic relationship. Both of us were divorced, both still healing, both very vulnerable, and neither had been looking for a love relationship. However, there was something undeniable, impossible for of us to ignore; we were definitely romantically drawn to each other.

Falling

However, the things running through our minds at the time were not the kind of thoughts that normally occur when a person is thinking about a new love relationship. I was not thinking about how handsome he was, about his very sexy eyes, or about his wonderful physique. I would later find out that he was not thinking about those things either. Our attraction went much deeper than the physical, beyond the emotional and into the spiritual. We felt connected to each other in a way that was indescribable. We both felt that we knew each other so well, so intimately; that at times we knew and understood the other's heart better than we sometimes understood our own. We felt that we were getting to know, understand, and deeply care about the essence of who each other was.

After our in-depth discussion—that was one of the things I loved about us; the fact that we could talk about anything, openly and honestly—we decided to see where our new path would lead us and were determined to take things one day at a time. Rene and I had decided to date—no, Rene was courting me!

BeeCause You Loved Me

As we were leaving to go to our respective cars, we hugged each other good-bye, and as we parted from our hug, Rene did something I did not expect. He kissed me. His lips, ever so gently, yet with a passion I would never have anticipated, connected with mine. I was shocked, as I did not expect the kiss at all, let alone the emotions. Rene stepped back, looked at me with those big, beautiful brown eyes of his (I said our attraction was on a deep spiritual level, but I did not say I was blind!), and searched my eyes. His eyes said, *Was it OK that I just did that?*

My response to the question in his eyes was an awed and stuttered, "You k-k-kissed me!" Yes, I know—my lack of love experience had once again prominently displayed itself.

Rene began to pull back, as if he had done something wrong, but I would not let him. I said, "I am sorry, I just did not expect it, but I am happy that you did."

He then ever so gently touched my cheek with the back of his hand and looked deeply into my eyes. That very intimate act, I would later find out, was something Rene would end up doing repeatedly in our relationship.

Falling

It was one of his many signs of affection toward me. His gentle yet intimate touch always had a way of grounding and balancing me.

We looked into each other's eyes, and I swear, there was no one and nothing else in the world at that time that mattered but us. The world around us seemed to fade into the background, and as I looked into his eyes, my stomach turned to butterflies, my heart skipped a beat, and I let out a slow, inaudible sigh.

We both had limited time, so the meeting was short, but there was a chemistry brewing between the two of us which we could not ignore. The kiss only confirmed what we had felt over time but had not, until that day, acted on. Not knowing quite what else to do, we agreed to meet again the next day. Now, that was not an easy task, as I lived in the Eastside area of Seattle and he lived more than fifty miles north of me, which, in rush-hour traffic, could sometimes take an hour and a half to two hours to commute. However, when people are starting to fall in love, traffic, commute times, and other obstacles just don't seem as daunting as they would otherwise. That's not to say there were not obstacles—there were.

After seeing each other that day, we later talked again for hours on the phone. We each discussed the events of our day, talked about ministry work we needed to complete, and of course shared our feelings about each other. It seemed that we never ran out of things to talk about, topics to explore, or opinions to share.

In order to understand our relationship, I must paint you a clear picture of the two of us. I will attempt to describe Rene first. He was a man with a gentle heart, a deep soul, and a love for God. He was a five-foot-ten, 185-pound, muscular man with salt-and-pepper hair (more pepper than salt; just enough to give him that George Clooney or Richard Gere distinguished look). He had the most incredible dark brown eyes with beautiful long eyelashes that no man should have a right to. And Rene's smile was amazing. When he smiled, he did not just smile with his lips, he smiled with his eyes and his spirit.

He laughed easily and loved deeply, but there was also this hidden part of him that he kept guarded. Rene's

Falling

heart had layers, kind of like an onion. What I call the "outer layer" of his heart was very open, where just about everyone he met was accepted and welcomed.

Then, he had the special place in his heart that was one layer deeper, which was reserved for close friends and extended family. The next layer deep was one reserved for close family.

There were two more remaining layers. The part of his heart that I called the "cherished one" was the layer he reserved for the love of his life. Even that layer itself was somewhat like an onion, which was peeled back over time as he allowed himself to love, trust, and therefore open up more. It was the place where he loved deeply and hard. It was also the place where Rene held his past wounds from previous hurts and joys from new love. That layer was complex, beautiful, and sometimes frightening, because once I reached that part of his heart, I realized how much this man could love, how deeply he could hurt, and how unique a human being he was.

BeeCause You Loved Me

The last layer of Rene's heart was one that I knew I would never see. It was reserved for one person only, and no one else would ever go there. It was what I called "the God layer." It was a place where he communed with God, and God alone. Rene reserved this place for his spiritual time with the Lord. It was a layer of his heart which long ago had been set aside, when he became a Christian in his early twenties and gave his heart to God. That layer made the man, the husband, the father, the minister, and the prophet. It was the "essence" of Rene.

It was all those layers that made up the beautiful person of Rene, which began to capture my heart. And, if there really is such a thing as "falling in love," then I tripped, staggered, and fell head over heels in love with that incredible man.

4

Dating

Rene and I began spending more time together. Whether it was going out to dinner, to the movies, or just sitting on the couch and watching television, we began to make a concerted  effort to manage our schedules so that we could spend as much time together as our demanding lives would permit.

We also continued all our ministry work, writing books, ministering at different churches, and the like. We were courting, but we were also growing Rene's ministry together. Things were very good between us; however, there were some odd things that started occurring with me at the same time.

I remember the first time I was scared—well, actually, frightened—while I was with Rene. It was something I will never forget, and was one of the critical things that occurred in our relationship that changed me forever.

I was going through a very stressful time, and it was at the beginning of our dating phase. Rene was in the Eastside area and stopped by my house to visit. I had an appointment and had come home from work early, and Rene and I had decided to meet at my house since he was already in the vicinity. We had not planned to see each other until later on that week, so of course I was excited to see him. However, at the same time, I was tired and stressed because I had so many things going on. It was not one of my better days.

Dating

The two of us seeing each other that day was just a little while after our first kiss. However, after that first kiss, we had refrained from being very affectionate with each other, as we wanted to slowly build our relationship.

I was exhausted from challenges I was facing at work, as well as things that were going on with my ex-husband and kids, and I felt like I had hit a wall.

Rene took one look at me and he could tell. So he sat down on the couch at an angle, with his back to the corner, one leg up on the couch and the other on the floor, and said, "Come here. Sit down for a minute and relax."

I sat down, leaned my back against his chest, and lay the back of my head on his shoulder. Rene wrapped his arms around me, and reached up with one hand and caressed my forehead and face. This was the first time Rene had really held me, and when he did, something happened that terrified me more than words could ever explain.

BeeCause You Loved Me

I felt myself emotionally yield to him. The scary thing was that this was not a conscious yielding on my part. I had no idea that I had put up so many emotional shields, walls, and barriers. I was very surprised to discover that they not only existed, but that they were dissolving, all at the same time.

This undulation of emotions occurred just from this man simply touching and holding me. My initial reaction was to jump up off the couch. That is, until I realized that my stress had begun to dissipate, and that there was something about Rene, about our relationship, about "us," that made me feel totally and completely safe.

This feeling was an incredible milestone for us—and me—because it was then that I realized I had never experienced this feeling of "safety" before with a man.

Feeling safe, both physically and emotionally, was something that sometimes escaped me because I had been physically and sexually abused as a child.

The age of five is my first memory of being violated by a man. And at that moment, with Rene, I began to

Dating

realize that feeling safe with men was not something I had ever really experienced.

I had a stepfather that was physically and sexually abusive, and a male cousin had abused me until the time I was twelve. Their violation of my innocence had taken away my ability to trust overall, especially men.

What I did not know prior to this moment with Rene was that I had no reference point for male and female trust relationships, and until then, I had not known that such wonderful feelings of security, trust, and love could exist with a man.

If you have ever heard anything about female victims of sexual and physical abuse, as we become adults, we unfortunately (and sometimes unconsciously) seek out relationships with men that repeat the paradigm in which we grew up.

Sadly, my first husband only reinforced that very notion to me because he was also physically and emotionally abusive.

BeeCause You Loved Me

So, to find my protective shields melting at the hand and touch of this man was extremely disarming, but at the same time, nothing less than an incredibly freeing phenomenon that changed both our relationship and me forever.

Rene's love was breaking my protective shell. Rene's love had freed my caged bird and my spirit. I was caged and did not know it; I was shackled and thought that everyone's movements were as restricted as mine. My life experiences had taught me that what I had experienced as a child and an adult was reality. What I had not known was that my reality was an incorrect picture of the world, life, and love. This love was capturing me, shattering my incorrect picture, and repainting the world for me on a new canvas.

The next few weeks were like a whirlwind. We met and saw each other when we could, gathering "moments" here and there, which was sometimes difficult due to the distance between our two homes. However, somehow we managed to see each other several times a week, and especially on Sundays and Wednesdays.

Dating

Sundays were days we knew we would see each other. The kids and I would drive to Rene's church fifty miles north, and then we and many of the parishioners would all go out to brunch together. It was wonderful spending time worshipping together and being in church. I loved hearing him minister God's word. His messages, the prophetic words God gave him, and his tender heart toward the Lord, were such wonderful things. Rene was an incredible minister, with an ability to hear and speak the prophetic word of the Lord. The messages he preached were thoughtful, insightful, and caused one to contemplate God, His word, and His purpose in one's life in different and new ways.

My teenage children ended up becoming part of a youth group and worship team near Rene, so on Wednesday afternoons I would pick them up and drive north to take them to worship practice and their youth service. The practice and service spanned several hours, and it did not make sense for me to drive fifty miles back home and return to pick them up, ending up driving two

BeeCause You Loved Me

hundred miles in one night, so over time, Wednesdays became "date night" for Rene and me.

Those Wednesdays are precious memories that I will forever cherish. They were "our time." We agreed on no interruptions, no cell phones, just time for us to spend with each other. What a wonderful blessing that commitment we made to each other became as it carried on throughout our relationship.

I would drop the children off at their practice, and Rene would meet me somewhere in the north end after work. We would oftentimes have dinner, go to a movie, or just spend time talking. Our favorite time of year for date night was the time between summer and late fall.

During those wonderful summer and fall days, we spent our time at parks, near lakes, or doing something that allowed us to be outdoors and near water.

We kept blankets and pillows in our cars and had impromptu picnics—spreading out our blankets to sit on, eating, enjoying the outdoors, and listening to the sounds of birds singing, children playing, and water moving.

Dating

It was the first time in my life that I had actually "stopped and smelled the roses." I never knew how much I enjoyed the outdoors until I discovered it with Rene. We would laugh, talk, and enjoy each other's company. We also loved to just cuddle and hold each other.

Oftentimes, we would watch the sun set at a park that was on top of a hill and overlooked a large lake. During those date nights, we saw some of the most beautiful sunsets I have ever seen.

As we watched the sun disappear beyond the hills and mountains, we would look into each other's eyes and talk about our deepest emotions, our greatest fears, our hopes and dreams, our disappointments and shortcomings, and our desires and preferences. Some of the most precious conversations were when we did not have to speak at all.

We had the unique ability to be able to communicate with each other at times without saying a word. Our touch, holding each other, or just being in each other's presence oftentimes spoke volumes.

BeeCause You Loved Me

Little did I know at the time that this special connection and method of nonverbal communication would prove to be an indispensable lifeline for us in the future.

Never before in my life had I experienced such an incredible sense of connectedness. Our love seemed at times almost more than either of us was able to contain. It overflowed and overwhelmed our hearts in such a way that both pleased and surprised us. We often discussed the fact that although I was in my late thirties and Rene was in his mid-forties, with an eleven-year age difference between us, we often felt like teenagers falling in love. Never in our lives had we felt so alive, so free, and so loved.

I do not know even how to convey our love and feelings in a way that would portray them justly. To say that our love was bigger than us is an understatement; it was truly the essence of true agape love. We loved each other unconditionally—for everything we were, everything we were not, and everything we had been; the good, the bad, and the ugly—and we loved each other for what we were then, what we could and would be, and for all the mistakes we would make along the way as we grew together.

Rene would look at me with those incredibly big brown eyes, and his look would penetrate my shell, past my outer me, straight to the depths of my heart. He would then say, "I adore you." Moreover, his actions matched his words. No one (except God) had ever known me or been able to read me, understand my moods, comfort my fears, reassure my doubts, or love me the way Rene did. I knew that he loved me—no matter what I did, no matter what I said. Even when I was a disappointment to myself, he stilled loved me. I didn't have to "perform" for him, as you have to do in some relationships. I didn't have to try to be something I was not; his love allowed me to just be me. At the same time, he challenged me to become the best "me" I could be, but Rene never ever asked me to become anything other than the "me" God created me to be.

BeeCause You Loved Me

It was through Rene's love that I began to open my heart, my life, my mind, and my spirit in ways which I never knew were an option. This inexplicable connection we had is what propelled us into our relationship and motivated us to continue our endeavor of walking in true love.

We continued to date and to get to know each other. We began to spend more and more time together. We discovered that the more time we spent with each other, the more time we wanted to spend. We discovered that we could talk on the phone for hours and hours at a time, and never run out of things to say. We discovered that there were times when we did not have to say anything to each other because we already understood and knew what the other was feeling. In the midst of our dating and ultimately courting, we discovered that there was hope.

We also discovered something interesting about ourselves. We discussed the fact that we had previously been married to people that understood how to take from us, but, due to no fault of their own, were not able to give very much. This delta between giving and receiving had caused us both to have extremely depleted love banks, and we realized that we had spent our entire adult lives in a love deficit. We had forgotten how it was to "receive" from someone. In our entire adult lives, and even during our youth, we had never had the opportunity to be in a reciprocal relationship—which ours was—and it felt wonderful.

Do you have any idea what it was like to go from giving, giving, giving, and hoping, and accepting any little morsel of love the other person was willing to give? What it was like to spend years, even decades, in a relationship where you had to shut down your emotions just to survive? What it was like to be in a relationship where you did not even know that you were unhappy? Where you had become resigned to the notion that your marriage and reality didn't get any better than this?

If you answered yes to any of these questions, then you know and understand what a gift, blessing, and incredible miracle it was to have an opportunity to find true love, and to meet your life partner. If you understand this, then you understand the depth of our caring, the fast growth of our relationship, and the undeniable bond that we began to establish.

So, upon the realization that our relationship was indeed something special that we had been blessed with, we discussed many things. We talked about our families, our children, our ex-spouses, and about the impact our relationship would have on everyone.

Rene and I knew that we had some challenges; blending families is never easy, and blending multicultural families is even more difficult. Rene was first-generation Mexican American, and I am African American. For the two of us, race, color, etc., were not an issue. We saw people for who they are, the essence of them, not the color of their skin or the cultural background. I would later find out that among our races, there were still many people on both sides that could not get past the amount of pigment in our skin.

Although my ex-husband was in the process of getting ready to remarry, there were still challenges. And, although Rene's boys were basically adults, I was not the

Dating

type of person they pictured their father with. So, we evaluated the challenges, anticipated some of the issues, and decided that it is rare for anyone to ever find this kind of love. We knew that most people live a lifetime in relationships just trying to make them work. We knew from experience that what we had was different. We had found our soul mates, and for that, we were willing to take on the challenges, roll with the punches, and work through the difficulties.

Because Rene and I had both married young the first time (and both to people we met while in high school), we wanted—no, **needed**—to be able to make a love decision that was healthier and more mature—for us, for our children, and for our families.

We also wanted a second chance to show our children (five in all) what true love was like. Because of the impact of our previous marriages, we wanted to show them what a happy, healthy, and loving relationship looked like. We wanted to provide them the opportunity to experience the positive effects of a reciprocal, respectful, giving and caring love relationship. So that as they grew older and began their lives, they would have a living example of what a healthy relationship was like.

And, we wanted to share our love. We were beginning to find that our love was somewhat contagious.

Wherever Rene and I went, whether it was out to dinner, the movies, grocery shopping, or running errands, it seemed that our love was contagious. Something about our relationship and interaction caused people to smile and to want to be around us. We were known by name at restaurants, and even had favorite tables and servers who sat with us.

I know this sounds like a fairy tale, but it is true. In each other, we had found our soul mates, and it showed. I transformed into a different person. No, I transformed into *me*. The person I had been before was a shell of me; because of this relationship and our love, I was able to truly be *me*, and I cannot begin to tell you how freeing that was.

Dating

The world seemed to be a different place. I was truly a different person, and it was good. So good that my teenage son and daughter told me one night, "Mom, we really like the new you."

I said, "What do you mean?"

"We like the new you. The way that you are now is so much different than how you were with Dad."

"Really? How am I different?"

"Well, you are just different. The old Mom did not laugh that much, you were much more uptight back then, and you weren't happy. We never could have even had this talk with you or told you that back then, but we can now. We love being around you, hanging out with you, talking to you. We couldn't be that way with the old you."

Straight from the mouths of babes. Hey, I knew I was feeling different, I knew I was happier, I knew I was in love and had found my soul mate, but what I did not know was that the transformation I felt taking place in my heart, mind, and spirit had transcended from my heart and penetrated through to create the "real" me.

BeeCause You Loved Me

The conversation I decided to have with my children that night is forever etched in my mind. I talked to them about how they felt about the divorce and how they felt about me dating. The discussion was enlightening, joyous, and incredibly sad. I had no idea that my marriage had caused so much unhappiness, not just to me, but also to my children. As I said before, I had no idea how unhappy I was, but I was starting to get a clear picture of who I had been. I was eternally grateful for what I was becoming, and in turn, what my relationship with my children was becoming. True love is truly amazing.

Knowing that our love, relationship, and connection was a once-in-a-lifetime opportunity, and truly a gift, we did what only made sense. We started talking about getting married!

5

Engagement

As the months went by, our love grew and our lives continued to blend. Rene's voice was the last one I would hear at night on the phone, and the first one I would hear in the morning. We talked every night before we went to sleep, and I could always count on my good morning phone call from him the next day.

It was so funny; we both talked about the fact that we felt like teenagers. I felt as if I were falling in love for the first time. I realized that I was "awakening."

BeeCause You Loved Me

I realized that the "real" me was coming out because I knew that I was unconditionally loved. I knew that no matter what happened, Rene loved me for me; for the essence of who I am. I knew he supported my strength, and he made me feel safe enough to share my vulnerabilities with him. I knew, beyond a shadow of a doubt, that I was inexplicably and unequivocally loved.

Everything we saw in our futures included each other. The alternative would seem to be unbearable for either of us, and we both knew that we wanted to grow old together. We were best friends, partners, lovers—soul mates—and we wanted to spend the rest of our lives together. We would sometimes discuss trying to visualize our lives without each other, and we just could not do it.

You know, I almost went right into telling you about us choosing when we would get married, and left out one of the best parts of this story: how Rene proposed to me!

It was Valentine's Day 2004, which was a Saturday. What was pleasantly unusual about this particular Valentine's Day was that, although it was a bit chilly outside, it was beautiful here in Seattle. The sky was blue,

Engagement

the sun was shining, and for February, it was warmer than normal.

Rene told me I needed to be ready by nine a.m. on Valentine's Day, and that he would pick me up. Nine o'clock in the morning? On a Saturday, and Valentine's Day? OK, anyone reading this book right now who knows me is probably falling over laughing because of my "Saturday Rule": Do not contact me before eleven a.m. on a Saturday. Do not text me, do not call my cell phone or home phone, and definitely *do not* ring my doorbell. It is the one day of the week that I can sleep in, and I look forward to it every week. No exceptions. Saturdays are my lazy days, at least until noon.

Laugh if you will, but this rule was serious business. So, you can imagine the look on my face when Rene told me that I needed not only to be up before eleven a.m., but ready by nine. And, it was in that moment that I knew it really must be love, because the words I heard coming out of my mouth and the silly grin on my face both said, "Yes, I will be ready." Go figure.

BeeCause You Loved Me

The thought of starting our Valentine's Day together early meant so much to me. I wanted to spend the day of love and romance with the love of my life. He could have asked me to be ready at six a.m. and I would have been. Well, actually, six would have been pushing it. I guess there are limits, even to our special love!

In the early hours of February 14, 2004, I got up and prepared for the day with my love. I never knew that love could feel this way. The only thing he would tell me was to make sure I brought something warm to either wear or put on. So, I readied myself for the day by putting on one of the outfits I knew he loved.

In addition, I made sure that the Valentine's Day presents I had gotten him were ready, so that I could give them to him when he arrived. We loved to give each other very expressive and heartfelt greeting cards.

We often underlined specific words in the cards that meant a lot to us, and then would write very endearing and sentimental things to each other. Sometimes we used up all the blank space inside the cards to convey our love, appreciation, and affection to each other.

Engagement

This Valentine's Day was no exception. I gave him two cards. One was not enough. I needed to express to Rene how much I loved him, not only as a lover, but also as my best friend. There was nothing I could not share with him; no emotion was too powerful or so scary that I could not express it. My heart was safe, and I knew it. My heart had found a home, a place in which it could safely reside. I knew I was blessed, and wanted him to know that I understood we had something that most people never have the opportunity to experience in a lifetime.

What I would discover later is that this wonderful man saved every card I ever gave him. Quite a few cards, as we often did not wait for holidays or special occasions to express our love for each other via this venue. And on many occasions, we gave them to each other "just because."

I had the cards, a gift, some balloons, and other things ready for my sweetheart when he arrived. That morning when he came to pick me up, he brought me long-stemmed red roses, candy, a card, and several gifts. But that was not all.

He said, "OK, we need to go so we will not be late."

Late? I thought. OK, where in the world could we be going that we would be "late" at nine a.m.? I soon found out.

Rene was so excited. As he drove, we talked, laughed, and held hands like we usually did. I soon began to realize that we were heading toward downtown, and then I realized we were headed to the pier.

One of the most alluring elements of the Puget Sound area in Seattle is the surrounding natural beauty. We have Puget Sound, Lake Washington, Mt. Rainier, Mt. Baker, Snoqualmie Falls, beautiful green parks, beaches, forests, and much more. One does not have to travel far to get to some kind of natural beauty and escape from the hustle and bustle of day-to-day living. It is one of the reasons that people come here on business or for a vacation and end up returning later to live here.

Engagement

I would venture to say that the majority of people who live in Washington State are what we natives call "transplants." They were born elsewhere, lived in some other state, and at some point in their lives moved here.

Me? I am one of the few native Washingtonians. Born and raised here in Washington. When people discover this, they often look at me and say, "You were born here? You have lived here all your life?" My response? "Yep."

I have traveled to many places all over the world, and though I am currently contemplating moving to another state, I will admit that I have not found anywhere else that offers the diversity of scenery in such close proximity as Washington does.

The pier or waterfront is where our ferries arrive and depart, as well as what we call specialty boats. It also now has dedicated terminals, where most of the major cruise lines arrive and depart.

We got to the pier, and by then I was really wondering what he was up to. What could we be doing here so early in the morning? Then I thought, *Oh, he is probably taking me on a ferryboat ride over to one of the islands, and we are going to spend the day there.* We had done this before and really enjoyed it.

Wrong.

Rene had something better in mind. We arrived, he parked the car, and with excitement in his voice and a mischievous look in those gorgeous brown eyes, he led me over to an area reserved for one of the specialty ships.

"What are you up to?" I asked.

"Just wait and see," he responded.

When we got over there I saw the sign: Smooth Jazz Valentine's Day Cruise. We had been on one of these types of ships before for my birthday, and I had loved it. I love the water; being on it, the sound of it, watching it, listening to it. There is something about water—its movement, its power, its ability to push, pull, and propel—that is very calming to me, and Rene knew it. And once again, Rene had paid attention to the little things about me and had hit the jackpot with this cruise. And the cruise was only part of his surprise.

Engagement

It was a lover's cruise, lasting several hours, complete with wonderful, live music. What I did not know was that there was a destination involved as well!

As we boarded the boat, we stopped at the gangway to get our pictures taken. I still have those photos. Rene and I standing there, his arm around me, huge grins on both our faces, and me holding a single red rose near my cheek.

We listened to music, and then decided to go upstairs and outside, to look at the Sound from the top deck. Rene's arm around me, we stood there soaking in the beauty of the day: the blue sky, the sun, and the breeze, which was still a little cold. But that did not matter, because my heart was warmed.

This man had taken inventory of the things I loved, and wrapped them all up in one package for me in the form of a cruise, just because he loved me. The cruise, the water, and the live music were all beautiful.

As those infomercials say, "But wait, there's more!" We arrived at our destination and I was almost in tears. It was an island, and on it was a beautiful natural log conference center. It had lush green lawns and beautiful plants, and the building's architecture was wonderful. The design of the building was a tribute to our Native American roots here in Washington. The entire island project had been built with the focus of respecting and highlighting the natural beauty.

We walked into the conference hall of the log building to find it beautifully decorated in red, white, and pink. There were dining tables set with white tablecloths and pink and red accents of napkins and designs on each table. There were red and pink roses in vases on each table and throughout the building, as well as pink, red, and white balloons; every detail was structured to focus on conveying love and celebrating Valentine's Day.

We had lunch there, and the food was amazing. We had grilled salmon, which is one of my favorites, asparagus (my favorite vegetable) in this incredible sauce, all kinds of other vegetables, sides, salads, entrees, and desserts, including cheesecake.

Engagement

I looked at my man with tears in my eyes and all I could say was, "Thank you, baby. I love you."

We dined, talked with other couples, enjoyed our wonderful lunch, and then had some time to walk around the grounds alone together. We walked, talked, held hands, soaked in the natural beauty of the surroundings, and basked in the beauty of our love. We knew our love was special, and the entire day he planned said just that: "I love you."

After lunch, we boarded the boat and listened to the live smooth jazz love songs being played on the way back.

Upon returning to the pier, we picked up several copies of the picture taken when we boarded and then set off to walk back to the car.

By this time, it was probably around five p.m., and Rene asked, "Did you like your day?"

I said, "Baby, how could I not? I loved my day, and I love you. Thank you for making this Valentine's Day so special."

BeeCause You Loved Me

He smiled at me, kissed me, and said, "It's because I love you so much. You deserve it. You are worth it."

With the evening still ahead of us, we decided to go to Alki Beach, which is a fifteen- to twenty-minute drive from the waterfront. Alki is located in West Seattle and has a very long stretch of beach, right next to Puget Sound.

We decided to take a romantic stroll along the beach and spend more time listening to the water and smelling that wonderful combination of sand, open air, and sea.

By this time it was relatively dark. The nights here are long and the days are short at that time of year. The sun had gone down and it had gotten colder, but we decided to walk for a little while anyway. The view was amazing; there were lights that illuminated the walkway on the beach. With it being a clear day, there was no cloud cover, which made it colder as night fell, and gave us one more reason to wrap our arms around each other and snuggle as we walked.

Engagement

Rene and I decided to stop at a point, to look at the water and hold each other. It was colder by the water, and Rene asked me to let him know when it was getting too cold for me so that we could head back to the car.

After about fifteen minutes of standing there, in spite of the fact that he was holding me, I was getting chilled. I told him, "OK, I am starting to get a little cold, but I want to stay a little longer."

He responded, "OK." Now, up until this point, we had only been *talking* about the fact that we knew we wanted to get married. We had even gone looking at rings and had picked out ours, but we had skirted around the conversation that would make it official.

He then asked me, "Are you sure that you still want to marry me someday?"

I said, "Yes."

"You're sure?"

"Yes," I responded, as my teeth began to chatter.

BeeCause You Loved Me

Then, he pulled something out of his coat pocket and got down on one knee, and Rene said this:

"Then, Monique, will you please do me the honor of becoming my wife? Will you marry me?"

This incredible man, down on one knee, was looking at me with those big, beautiful brown eyes, and in that sexy voice of his was truly asking me to be his wife!

"Yes! Yes! Yes!" I said, with tears in my eyes, holding his face and kissing him. He got up, opened the ring box, and put my engagement ring on my finger. We embraced and kissed, and then I said loudly to anyone that was listening, "I LOVE THIS MAN!"

OK, now you have to understand why I did that. At the time, a TV commercial was airing that made Rene and I both tear up every time we saw it. As a matter of fact, sometimes he would be at his house, I would be at mine, the commercial would come on, and one of us would call the other and say, "Turn to (channel), our commercial is on."

Engagement

This commercial depicted a man in an open square, down on one knee proposing to a woman, and then, after they embraced, picking her up and swinging her around while she responded loudly, "I love this man! I love this man! I love this man!"

Now you understand why I had to say it, if for no other reason than the fact that we were both hopeless romantics and it was the perfect culmination to a beautiful day.

We walked back to the car arm in arm, knowing that we had officially decided that we were going to spend the rest of our lives together.

Later that evening, we went out to dinner to celebrate our love, and then called everyone we knew to tell them that we were engaged!

We also began discussing when we should we get married. We wanted to start our new life. We loved spending time together, after almost a year of commuting back and forth, especially in rush-hour traffic, the hundred-plus-mile round-trips to see each other were becoming a little tiresome.

We also looked at economics; we were supporting two households, and it just did not make sense to continue doing that for a long period of time. And, we were both grown—we were not teenagers, or even in our early twenties. I was thirty-four and Rene was forty-five. Of course, all those "supporting arguments" were just our way of saying that we wanted to start the rest of our lives together sooner rather than later. So, we decided to get married in May. Not May of the following year—that year. May 2004 was just three months away!

6

Wedding

By the Monday after the Valentines' Day weekend, the reality began to sink in. We had a wedding to plan! There were tuxedos to pick, a church to find, a reception to determine, people to select for the wedding party, a wedding dress to choose, colors to decide on, and...oh my! Clearly, I needed to create a project plan and schedule for my wedding.

I run program management offices for a living. My life had been in technology and the software industry for a long time, so I did what I knew how to do best. I determined how I was going to manage the fact that Rene and I were getting married in a little over three months, and would need to find a new house, pack up both our homes, and move—all within that time frame. Yes, a project schedule was definitely needed!

I had never had so much fun in my life. When I went back to work that Monday after Rene proposed, I was almost giddy. All the women in the office noticed my ring and my huge smile right away. The enthusiasm of people that I had just started working with a few weeks before was absolutely amazing.

The wedding planning made Rene and I feel like we were kids again. Watching us together as we decided on invitations, colors, cakes, flowers, etc., you would have thought that neither of us had been through this process before. Something about the love we had found with each other made it all new and refreshing, and a wonderful experience for us both.

Now, since I am not writing a fairy tale, I do not want you to think that with all the stress of a new job, packing, moving, designing a wedding dress, planning a wedding,

Wedding

and so on, that Rene and I were "lovey-dovey" all the time. We were most of the time; however, there were times when stress got to the both of us. The long commute to see each other added to the stress. We were raising our children, writing ministry books, and planning a wedding, and sometimes we were just plain exhausted.

During that time, we sometimes would just stop all the planning and everything we were doing, sit on the couch, snuggle, and watch a movie. We knew there were times when we needed to "reconnect" and remember the real goal of why we were doing everything, and that was to be together.

I have never known of a man that wanted to be so involved in his wedding. Typically, when it comes time for a bride and groom to select invitations and determine colors, one hears complaints from the bride-to-be that the groom-to-be does not show enough interest. Well, that was not the case with our wedding. Rene wanted to be a part of everything, of every decision. From sitting for several hours looking through mounds of wedding invitation books, to meeting with the florist to select the flowers, to looking through wedding magazines with me to pick the style of cake we wanted—Rene was right there. This was *our* wedding, and he made sure that I knew how excited he was to be marrying me. How did I manage to be so blessed?

The other wonderful thing about our selection process was that Rene and I had very similar tastes. We liked the same colors, textures, styles, and types of food, so our discussions around choices for the wedding were rarely, if ever, based on disagreements. We never had to "compromise" on a selection because our tastes were so similar; instead, we often would pick the same thing at the exact same time.

By the time our wedding day came, like many brides to be, I was exhausted! A ministry friend of ours designed and made my wedding dress, which fitted me and was perfect. It was an ivory colored dress, with deep burgundy lace around the bottom and the top of the bodice, and the train was of burgundy lace. It was absolutely beautiful. I felt and looked like a princess in it. My veil had

Wedding

flowers in it the same color as the lace on the dress and was partially a tiara. I was indeed a princess, but not only for the day. I knew I was Rene's princess for life.

Our wedding was beautiful. Rene's tuxedo was black, with a vest and bow tie of burgundy that matched the lace and bodice on my dress.

Our flowers and cake matched our colors, and the whole church spoke of love. We were finally getting married!

The pastor of the church was a long-time friend of Rene's. It was a lovely church, with wooden pews and with soft lighting. The beautiful paneled wall behind the pulpit was color decorated with two kissing doves and lace connecting them underneath.

We had golden candelabras holding eight burgundy candles on either side of the pulpit, representing new beginnings for both of us. We had determined that we also wanted to take communion, so a table on the altar was prepared for us to do so. Flowers decorated the pews and the altar.

BeeCause You Loved Me

Rene and I wanted to keep the wedding party small and intimate, so my mother was my matron of honor and my daughter was my only bridesmaid. On Rene's side, his son Jordan was his best man, and his brother Steve and my son Joshua were both attendants.

The main song for our wedding was "Because You Loved Me" by Celine Dion. If you have not heard the song, it is a beautiful testament of love. Part of the lyrics are: "I am who I am because you loved me / you were my strength when I was weak / were my voice when I couldn't speak." I had no idea that many of the words in the song were prophetic for our marriage and would end up being more than just a sentiment; that they would soon become my reality.

All the hard work and preparation had finally paid off. As I sat in a room with my mother, daughter, and friend while the photographer took pictures to document our special day, I could not have been happier.

My family helped me with the final touches of putting on my veil, fixing my burgundy lace train, and giving me the final once-over. When all that was done, it was finally time.

I was ready to meet my best friend, confidant, pastor, prophet, and lover at the altar to become his wife. It was time for me to walk down the aisle to meet Rene.

It was such an amazing feeling. I felt as if I had never done this before, and there was a sense of calm and peace around me. I was getting ready to walk down the aisle to become one with Rene, before God, our friends, and our families.

As the wedding march played and I began to walk down the aisle with my son, I saw friends and family on both sides smiling at me. I knew that I looked like a princess. The entire atmosphere of the church, the decorations, and the garments we wore all symbolized one thing—the special love Rene and I had for each other.

I looked ahead down the aisle, and there he was. Standing there looking as handsome as ever, waiting for me to meet him at the altar. Rene had a look in his eyes that is hard to describe. It was a look of love, anticipation, care, excitement, and peace. It seemed as if the look on both our faces said, "Finally, our day is here."

Once we reached the end of the runner, my son and I stopped and did as we had been instructed by the photographer. We turned around to face the church, still arm in arm, for the photographer to get a picture of my son walking me down the aisle.

After the photo, the officiating minister said, "Who gives this woman away?"

My daughter, Tyeshia, and my son, Joshua, both responded, "We do!"

At that point, Rene walked over to where Joshua and I were standing, Joshua relinquished my arm, and Rene took it. As Rene looped his arm in mine, with a big grin on his face, he leaned over and whispered in my ear, "Hi there!" This made me giggle, of course.

Our ceremony was an hour long, full of music, scriptures, and words of wisdom given to us by many of our pastor friends. I will not recount all the details; however, there a few key things I want to share so that

Wedding

you can visualize how wonderful and intimate our wedding day was.

Rene and I had decided that we were going to write our vows. We wanted to express our care, love, affection, and commitment to each other in our own words. So, we each wrote our own and agreed that we would not hear what the other person had written until we were standing at the altar on our wedding day.

As Rene began to say his vows, he began with this: "Monique, I promise to mow the lawn, take out the trash, and clean the garage." And the whole church broke out in laughter.

I started giggling, of course, and could not stop. Leave it to my dear sweet husband to be the one to bring some levity to the ceremony. I should have seen that coming!

He then said, "Oops, that's the wrong list. That is the honey-do list!" And again, more laughter.

Rene then lifted my veil, looked deeply into my eyes, and began to convey his wedding vows to me. He told me how much he loved me; how before meeting me he never thought he would be able to love again; how he had given his heart to me, and much more. In the midst of reciting his vows, he had to stop because he began to choke up.

The love in Rene's eyes, the sincerity of his voice, and the passion of the words he spoke cut straight into my heart and caused me to realize just how much this man loved me, and reiterated just how much I loved him.

Upon completing his vows, I do not know if there was a dry eye in the church, including mine, which made it that much more difficult for me to get my vows out without turning into "the blubbering bride."

What was amazing about our vows was that, hearing them, one would have thought we had written them together. Our words of love and commitment were so similar that it seemed as if we had written them in tandem, so much so that some were the same exact phrases. It was just another testament to how our hearts and spirits were in accord.

I had chosen to wear a corset underneath my wedding dress. You know, those things you would see

Wedding

women putting on in the old Western movies, with strings that went through holes and the body of it wrapped around the torso and "uplifted the girls." They were also known for making women pass out if they were too tight because they could not breathe in them. To say that a corset Is effective at slimming one's waist and uplifting other areas is true, and to say that it makes it difficult for a person to have free movement from the hips up is an understatement.

Knowing this will help you visualize what happened at the end of the ceremony. At the part where we were officially deemed husband and wife, and the minister pronounced us "Mr. and Mrs. Rene Munoz," Rene immediately grabbed me to kiss me.

However, in typical Rene fashion, he did not just wrap his arms around me and kiss me. He decided that he was going to dip me. Now, dipping requires the ability of the torso to bend, and remember, I had on the tight-fitting and unyielding corset. There was no room for me to bend. So, instead of a "dipping," what we got was more of a "tipping." Rene attempted to do such a dramatic dip that, in the process, he almost dropped me and we nearly fell over. After the shock, we both laughed hysterically. That began our new life together, as we walked down the aisle to exit the sanctuary as Mr. and Mrs. Rene Munoz.

I was his wife!

7

Marriage

We spent our wedding night in a beautiful rustic hotel in downtown Seattle, enjoying each other, our love, and the fact that we were both totally and completely exhausted. We had to get up and be ready to leave by six the next morning, to catch our flight to Cabo San Lucas for our honeymoon.

Neither of us had ever been to Cabo, so it was an adventure for us. It was an item on something we called our "firsts" list. While we were dating, we had made a list of things we wanted to do together which both of us had never experienced. The list was comprised of everything from water skiing, to going to Paris, to taking ballroom dancing lessons. The only two requirements for adding an item to the list were: 1) it had to be something neither of us had ever done before, and 2) it had to be something we wanted to experience together.

So, Cabo was on the "firsts" list. Our honeymoon was amazing. We stayed at a hotel where the rooms were actually part of the sand dunes, which ended up making it a wonderfully cooler room during the hot May days. We had a private patio, which directly extended out onto the beach. We could see the beach and the ocean from our room and enjoy the beach in privacy if we wanted to.

Let's just say that our experience there in Cabo was marvelous. We had time alone to love each other, to sightsee, to ride on Sea-Doos in the water (which was so much fun!), to experience the local food, restaurants, and music, and to finally recuperate from our whirlwind engagement and wedding. We were there for six days, and my only regret is that we did not make it at least two weeks. Then again, I do not know if I could ever have had

Marriage

enough alone time with that man, no matter where we were!

The only glitch that happened was during the early morning after our last day. Rene had eaten from the salad bar in the restaurant we went to on our last night there, and I had not. I know, I know; you are thinking: He ate the salad? Doesn't he know that you are not supposed to eat the salad in countries like that because the vegetables are washed in the local water?

I didn't even think about it at the time. But by early the next morning, the day we were scheduled to leave, Rene was thinking about it—a lot. And let's just say that he spent more time in the bathroom than in the bed.

I felt so sorry for him. Rene was a strong man with a pretty hardy stomach that could handle spicy foods and other things. However, whatever had gotten into him was waging war, and winning!

As soon as the hotel's gift shop opened, I ran and got him some anti-diarrheal medication to help stop the madness. He took a double dose and was at least able to lie down on the bed and rest a little, while I packed up so that we would be ready for the car when it came to pick us up and take us to the airport.

I was worried, because the way he was looking and feeling made me wonder if he would be able to travel.

We had to get to the airport, go through security, check our luggage, go through customs, get on the plane, and then make through the almost five-hour trip home. With him requiring close proximity to a bathroom at a moment's notice, I was not quite sure how we were going to manage it. However, he assured me that he would be OK. He was not taking no for an answer—we were leaving as scheduled.

We had barely made it through airport security, when Rene had another "episode" and needed to find a restroom. The poor guy. The men's restrooms on the first floor were out of order and we had to go upstairs. I did not think he was going to make it. But, the man has the determination of Job to survive, so he made it.

Marriage

After that, we found him some chairs to lie down on and rest. I gave him some more medication, hoping to calm his stomach before we boarded the plane, made sure he had some fluids in him, and let him rest.

When we boarded the plane, our seats were right at the front, behind first class, so we did not have far to walk, thank goodness. We sat down, I put a blanket on him, and he rested his head on my shoulder and went to sleep.

It just so happened that we were sitting in a row of three across. I was sitting by the window, Rene was in the middle, and there was a woman in the aisle seat. She kept inquiring about Rene and how he was feeling, and when he was awake, asking him questions. It all seemed a bit odd, until she told us that she was a physician (an internal medicine doctor). How blessed we were! She told us what we needed to do, how to take care of it, and that he should see a doctor when we got back, to make sure that he had not acquired some parasite or bacterial infection. What a godsend!

BeeCause You Loved Me

Well, we made it home, safe and sound, and by the time we reached the house that evening, Rene was feeling better. I still made him go to the doctor the next day, just to be sure. He wasn't thrilled about that, but hey, that's what wives are for!

After we returned from the honeymoon, Rene and I began to settle in and get comfortable; to get in the groove with our lives.

We started our ministry school again and began holding lessons in our home, began writing our fourth ministry book, and continued traveling and ministering by speaking at conferences.

We did all that while holding full-time jobs—Rene in his roofing and remodeling business, and me in corporate America doing software development—and both of us raising my two teenagers.

Life was fun, though. We laughed as a family, played as a family, and just enjoyed the fact that he and I were married and finally living under the same roof. We put our desks in the same office in the house so that we could be near each other as we both worked on our respective business projects at home in the evenings, or as we were developing new or reviewing existing ministry materials in preparation for our speaking engagements or classes we were teaching. We also set up our office so it was central to the main part of the house.

When we moved into our home, we both knew we would have quite a significant amount of work to do on a regular basis, which would require computer work. We had work for the ministry—writing our teaching books, tests, and commentaries. Rene had his handyman work and hauling business with proposals, estimates, and invoices to generate, and I had work from my day job that often bled into the late hours of the night.

With all that working going on, we knew there would be some nights in which our time together would be extremely limited to sometimes nonexistent. And, we did not want to be away from each other, so we determined that we would make the family room our "office." It was large, with a fireplace, several tall windows, and space enough for two L-shaped desks, multiple computers and printers, and a television.

Our reasoning was that even though we had to work, we could still at least be in the same room, near each other, and close enough to steal a quick touch, hand holding, or kiss. And you know what? It worked! Just being in the same room gave us—well, I guess the best way to describe it is peace. We loved just being in each other's presence. We both laughed because we felt like we were more productive and efficient just being close to each other. Moreover, of course, we had an incentive— the sooner we completed our work, the more time we had to play, which included bedtime!

There were times in the summer where we both had significant work to complete after hours, and we would work until late in the evening. But, every once in a while during that time, Tyeshia and Joshua would come to us and say, "Can we please do a family movie night?" Oftentimes, we would look at each other, and the look in our eyes would be, *Why not? We have done enough work for a day.* So, we would tell the kids that we could, and

Marriage

have them go choose the movie, which was always a dangerous option. We never knew what we were going to get when it was their turn to pick the flick for movie night!

There were other times, however, when Rene and I really needed to address some unfinished work, or we were working against some tight deadlines. During these times, we would tell them how much we wanted to have an impromptu movie night, but could not.

Now, the rule in our house is that my kids have never asked twice once I have told them no. However, with Rene there, for some reason one night they pushed the issue. When Rene and I responded that we could not, but they could watch a movie if they wanted to, both kids said at the same time: "But, if we do a movie night, the two of you get to cuddle!"

Boy, did they know how to get our attention. Rene and I were the ultimate cuddlers. We were always touching each other. Another reason why our desks shared the same office—we wanted to be close. When this conversation with the kids happened, I remember thinking, *Boy, do they know how to get to us!* Cuddling was our Achilles' heel!

In that instance, Rene and I looked at each other and knew that our resolve to work had been depleted. We smiled, laughed, and said, "OK, guys, you got us! Give us half an hour and we will be there, but *we* get to pick the movie this time!"

After that night, it became one of our favorite family dynamics. Rene and I working, us saying, "No, we can't do a movie night," and the kids responding with, "But you can cuddle!"

It worked every time!

Thus began our life together as a family. We had barbecues with friends, family, and people from my work. We had birthday parties. We had people over almost every other Saturday for food, fun, fellowship, and to attend our ministry school.

We worked, we laughed, and we played. We had family pillow fights, and family tickle sessions. Well, actually, they were more like Rene tickle sessions, where we all ganged up on him. He hated being tickled, but laughed with us, always warning us by saying, "That's not funny! Somebody is going to get hurt, and I am very ticklish!" Which, of course, only made us tickle him more, and he knew it would.

Joshua and Rene would spend time doing the male bonding things that testosterone-based units do, such as working out, doing push-ups (all different varieties; one-handed, knuckle, etc.), lifting weights, going to one of the local athletic stores to get weights and other "manly" things, and just hanging out together in the garage or in the yard.

Sending the two of them to the grocery store, even with a specified list, was always a dangerous thing. It was very rare that they would return with all the items on the list actually purchased on the first trip. And, all too often they would return with many, many items that were not on the list and which usually did not provide very much nutritional value, such as varieties of candy, chips, nachos, and salsa. Ah, the men in my family. Go figure.

BeeCause You Loved Me

Times were good. The days began to get shorter, the leaves on the trees began to turn to those beautiful fall colors, and into a beautiful Indian summer, where the warmth of summer doesn't let go as fall arrives.

8

"Bee-Day"

As we moved into the month of October, Seattle's beautiful Indian summer continued and the weather was absolutely beautiful.

Beautiful sunrises, warm days and evenings, amazing sunsets. There was just enough breeze that it required us to wear a light jacket or sweater in the late evenings, but not so chilly that we didn't look forward to a nice walk or sitting outside on the patio to simply enjoy the evening. In the midst of this beauty, my mother was going through one of the ugliest things anyone ever has to face: death.

BeeCause You Loved Me

Not hers, thank God, but the impending death of her husband and my stepfather, Eddie. He had been ill for many years with heart disease. In and out of the hospital, and many nights and days I met my mother in the emergency room because he had suffered another heart attack. But his last episode, which had happened in September, had taken its toll. The end result had left him damaged beyond recovery and in a Persistent Vegetative State (PVS). He ended up in critical care, on a "vent," a breathing tube and machine to breathe for him. He eventually was taken off the breathing machine, moved to a regular room, and discharged to a care facility.

My mother kept hoping for a miracle, because over the years, God had been very merciful and Eddie had recuperated from seemingly impossible complications. However, this time everyone knew it was just a matter of time and he would soon pass away. Eddie's body had given out on him and was shutting down. And, on October 7, 2004, the hysterical phone call came from my mother, only several days after he went to the care facility. Eddie had died not long after she had left him that evening.

"Bee-Day"

Rene, the kids, and I rushed over to my mother's home very late that evening to be with and comfort her.

She was in no condition to handle all the things that would come, so I stepped in and offered to help. Actually, Rene and I told her that we would manage it all. She asked Rene to perform the eulogy, and she wanted me to sing. I offered to do the programs as well as get everything set up with the church.

I called into work the next morning to let them know Eddie had passed away. No one there was surprised, as I had kept them apprised of what was going on with him. I took the day off to be with my mother and help her with the arrangements. Eddie died on a Thursday, and I started making arrangements with my mother that Friday.

The following Monday, Rene and I went with my mother to the funeral home to discuss options and make arrangements. Her grief was almost palpable and the discussions were overwhelming for her.

Eddie had wanted to be cremated, and unlike in the movies where they discuss the "ashes" of your loved one, we were told as we sat there that they were not really ashes, but rather the remains of burnt bones. The temperature of the cremation oven was such that all flesh was burnt off and incinerated, and what she would receive as remains would basically be burnt bones. Morbid, I know, but true.

I tried to shield her from the unpleasant truth as much as possible by giving the mortician "the eye," which said, *Please shut up now, she doesn't need to know all those details.* And thankfully, he finally caught on and did shut up. Rene and I looked at each other, knowing that we were going to have to do something afterward to help my mother get through the day.

To try and get my mother's mind off it temporarily, Rene took us shopping. There was some perfume that my mother had wanted, and in typical loving Rene form, he bought us both everything we wanted, and then some.

While we were shopping, Rene and I would hold hands, and every once in a while, he would sneak a kiss in. My mother saw us and began teasing us, telling us to get

"Bee-Day"

a room! Rene responded with, "We have one, as soon as we get back home!"

My mother actually smiled and laughed while we were shopping. It was just another of Rene's amazing and wonderful attributes. He had the ability to turn any situation around—one of the many things I loved about him.

Rene went home, and I drove about an hour south to take my mother home. I spent the rest of the evening with her. After leaving, I drove the hour to our house, and was exhausted. I came home to find Rene working on the computer and looking as handsome as ever, as usual.

He had worked for the remainder of the day and was equally exhausted, but our evening was not close to being over. The memorial service would be on Wednesday, and I needed to finish the program so I could take it to the printer early Tuesday morning. Rene had work proposals and estimates to complete, so we both began working.

*Bee*Cause You Loved Me

So, the evening of October 11, 2004, we worked into the wee hours of the night; Rene on his business and me on Eddie's memorial service, obituary, and program.

When we finally finished, we were both beyond exhausted. So, we locked the house, turned off the lights, and headed upstairs to bed. We loved our bedroom. The walls were painted a burnt red and the wainscoting an antique white. We kept candles all over the room, and music playing all the time. We both loved music, and loved to make love and fall asleep to it. On this night, though, we changed into our nightclothes, climbed into bed, and let out a collective sigh.

We did something that night we had never done before; we lay down facing each other, looking into each other's eyes. Our typical routine was that I would lie on my left side and Rene would spoon me. I loved that feeling of him being close, of being safe, of feeling his love encompass me. I loved feeling him wrap himself around me, how tenderly and protectively he held me. I felt like he was keeping me safe in his personal cocoon. Until

"Bee-Day"

Rene, no one had ever spooned me. I did not even know what it was. Seriously!

You must be thinking: Wait a minute; I remember reading that she was previously married for sixteen years. You are correct, and no, I did not mistype that last paragraph. In sixteen years of marriage, I had never been spooned. Need I say more?

That evening, for some reason, we faced each other. Maybe because of the grief we had walked through with my mom that day, maybe because we had not spent that much time with each other in the previous few days, or maybe because mortality was looking at us in the face and the reality of how limited our time here on earth can be had impacted us both. Whatever it was, I found myself looking into those beautiful brown eyes with those wonderfully long eyelashes. With his head slightly bent on my chest so that he was looking up at me, I heard the love of my life ask:

"What would you do if for some reason I could not make love to you anymore?"

BeeCause You Loved Me

"Huh?" I said. The lights were still on, and I looked into his eyes quizzically.

His response was to ask again. "What would you do if I could not make love to you anymore?"

I said, "I would just continue to love you anyway. I love the essence of you and who you are. No matter what, I will always love you."

And his next question equally dumbfounded me. Although I thought the question was a little odd, due to the lateness of the hour and our tiredness, I did not think much of it—at least not at the time.

Rene asked, "Can you tell now when I say 'I love you' with my eyes?"

I looked deep into his gorgeous eyes, saw the love he had for me in them, and responded with an emphatic, "Yes!"

We fell asleep that way—my arms wrapped around him, his around me, with his head resting on my bosom. It was a sweet and wonderful sleep. Just being with the man

"Bee-Day"

I loved, trusted, honored, and adored. Knowing he loved me the same.

Morning came; it was Tuesday, October 12, and Rene had a half-day roofing job to do. He was helping a friend on a project and said he would be back home by early afternoon. I, on the other hand, stayed in bed for a little while. I was not going to work that day, as I was finalizing the arrangements for my stepfather's memorial service, which has happening the next day.

Rene kissed me good-bye, and I remember thinking, Man, I wish we had woken up in time for us to make love before he left. I rolled over and thought, *Hmmm…I will catch him tonight, when both of us are not so tired*. I felt like I just needed to feel him, love him, and hold him. Nothing new, I always did. For us, lovemaking was not just sex, and it was not just physical satisfaction. For us, lovemaking was a way we communicated our love and care for each other at the purest and most vulnerable emotional and spiritual levels. There were times when, in the midst of making love, that I truly felt as if we were on another spiritual plane with each other. The world seemed to fade, and it felt as if it was just the two of us, completely yielding and giving ourselves to each other. It was beautiful, and helped me understand even more the scripture verse which refers to two people becoming one. In those times, we were one. One in the flesh and one in the spirit, and it is something I will always be grateful that I experienced. As a matter of fact, that is how our lovemaking was most of the time. And no, I am not kidding or making this up. Our lovemaking was simply a physical representation of our emotional, intellectual, and spiritual connection. It was our way of communicating what words were incapable of expressing at times, the deep love we had in our hearts for each other. And it was beautifully amazing.

Now, back to the morning of October 12, 2004. I had my laptop in my room, and I sat up in bed to put the final touches on the program for the service before I hopped in the shower to get ready for the day. I had reached a point the night before where I just ran out of juice, and I knew it would be faster for me to finish the final touches in the morning, so that is what I started to do.

In the midst of finishing the program, one of my friends, Rondo, IM'd me.

Rondo, his partner, and I have been close friends for a very long time. He is one of those people who can make me crack up laughing at the drop of a hat. We share birthdays and special events together, and, well, we have walked through many things in life together. He is one of those people in my inner circle I call my "heart friends." The people that know the good, bad, wonderful, and ugly about me and choose to love me for who I am. He is one of the people in my life that is very close to my heart.

So, Rondo IM's me to see how my mother and I are doing, and in the midst of talking to him, another one of my heart friends comes online—Chris, but we call him Cheffe. So, the three of us end up in a three-way IM conversation. Typical for us. We all have worked at several places together and are very good friends. We met during our days of working at the largest software

BeeCause You Loved Me

company in the world in the nineties, and continued our friendship from there.

So, I am IM'ing them and telling them how happy I am with my life. How much I love Rene, and how happy our whole family is. They were commenting to me that they had never seen me so happy before, and how much they both really liked Rene. We discussed all of us and our spouses/partners getting together and either going out or having dinner at one of our homes. We cracked some jokes, laughed, and then said our good-byes. I love these people; they are truly gems and blessings in my life.

The next thing I knew, my cell phone was ringing. It was the friend that Rene went to work with, calling me.

Why was he calling me? Because. Because my life had changed forever, and I did not even know it yet. Because something so simple yet so profound had happened that would forever change Rene and everyone who loved him.

He called me *"Bee*Cause." *Bee*Cause Rene had been stung by a bee. *Bee*Cause about fifteen minutes after Rene had been stung by the bee, he had an allergic

"Bee-Day"

reaction and went into severe anaphylactic shock, which means his tongue began to swell and his airway began to close, blocking oxygen to his brain. *Bee*Cause Rene had collapsed on the roof, and they caught him before he fell when they heard him drop his shovel. *Bee*Cause the medics were there and were taking Rene to the hospital.

*Bee*Cause.

9

Emergency

The sky was blue, with not a cloud in it. Birds were singing, and people were going about their regular daily lives. Except for me.

I was driving. Driving about forty-five minutes from where we lived to the north end hospital where they had taken Rene.

I had talked to the medics; they told me what hospital they were taking Rene to and how to find the location. They were very nice, and I assumed that when I got there, I would see Rene sitting on the side of an

Emergency

emergency room bed, looking a little sheepish about the whole thing and waiting for me to take him home.

I expected that I would walk in, give him kisses, and tease him about how the little bee got the best of him. I figured that I would take him home, cook him his favorite meal (my absolutely fabulous meat loaf), spoil him for the evening, and remind him how much I loved him. All in a day's work for a wife, right?

Wrong.

I arrived in the emergency department, asked for my husband, and was led by a smiling nurse to his room. On the way there, she verified that I was Rene's wife and we chatted.

I was not prepared for what I saw when I stepped into that room in the ER. The love of my life was not sitting on the side of the bed, laughing and joking with the nurses and doctors. He was not sitting there looking sheepish. He was not sitting at all. Rene was lying on a gurney with tubes coming out of every part of his body.

BeeCause You Loved Me

Rene had been intubated. A tube had been placed in his mouth, down his throat, into his lungs, to breathe for him because he was unable to breathe on his own. And, he was not awake. He had heart monitor leads attached to his chest and a pulse oximeter tip on his finger. A monitor showed his vitals. And that darn breathing machine was going, making the sound which represents the fact that a person is unable to do the very thing that gives him or her life—breathe. The rhythmic yet disconcerting *ooosh-whoosh, ooosh-whoosh* sound of the breathing machine, reminding me that my husband was on life support.

Eerily enough, it was an exact replica of the last time my stepfather had been admitted to the emergency room. I had arrived with my mother at the hospital, and Eddie had been in the same condition as I now was seeing Rene. But this time, instead of my mother, it was me that I heard asking, "When is he going to wake up? When will the medications you gave him to paralyze him so that you could intubate him wear off?"

Emergency

Somehow, in the midst of my shock, I had forgotten that my mother had asked these very same questions, with me standing by her side, and I had known then, about Eddie, what I could not bring myself to even consider about Rene. Eddie wasn't going to wake up. And now, it was questionable whether Rene would either.

Not what I expected.

10

CCU

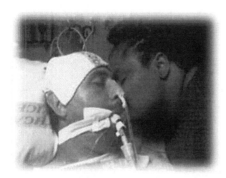

My family and friends say I called them and that the only way they knew it was me calling was because my number showed up on their phones. They say that they did not recognize my voice. I cannot tell you whether I sounded like myself or not, because I do not remember calling.

Every one of my friends and family can recount these phone conversations. I cannot. The only thing I remember is that the nurse told me they were moving Rene to the CCU (Critical Care Unit) right away, and that I should follow them. So I did.

There was a whirlwind of activities that happened when we arrived on the "Unit." That is what they (the clinicians) call the Critical Care Unit, or CCU. As I was soon to discover, a hospital has its own language. Not just regular medical lingo, but, just like any work culture, it has its own language, rhythm, and style.

What happened next, I cannot tell you exactly. Nurses came in and started "doing" things to my husband, and no one was talking to me. I stopped them. I said, "OK, I am his wife, and he is obviously unable to consent for care, so you need to ask me. First, what is going on? What is your treatment plan? Why are you giving him that medication, and what is it for?"

Well, that got their attention. *Oops, we stabilized him enough to move him from the ER, but we did not get consent from his wife.*

BeeCause You Loved Me

For everyone out there reading this, if you do not take anything else away from this book, please, please remember this: **YOU HAVE RIGHTS**. You have rights as a patient, and you have rights as a family member of a patient. You have the right for people to talk to you, to tell you what is going on, and to get your permission to do things. You have the right to say no. You have the right to get a second opinion. You have the right to ask questions, and to keep asking until they find a way to explain it to you so that you or your loved one understands. You have the right to question their recommendations, and you have the right to ask for a different caregiver if one is not working for you. You have the right to ask them for alternative solutions. You have the right to take time to think about what they are asking you to do. You have the right to be listened to, respected, and valued as a human being. **YOU HAVE RIGHTS**. Do not ever forget it. Nevertheless, sometimes clinicians and caregivers might, and you may have to remind them that you do.

All right. Back to the Unit. It is a unique organism in the hospital. It functions at a different pace than any

CCU

other hospital department. In most hospitals, most of the nurses on the Units are required to work twelve-hour shifts. This has to do with continuity of care for patients with critical and complex issues. Instead of three or four nurses in a twenty-four-hour period, a patient only has two. And, if the same two nurses are on for several days in a row, consistency of care is greatly improved.

On the Unit, each nurse typically does not have more than two patients. And, if a patient has an even higher acuity level (level of direct care required) than others on the Unit, a nurse may only have the one patient—that is, in most hospitals.

This one was different. *Very different*. Let us just say that it was not one of the premier hospitals in our region. They don't take gunshot wounds, stabbings, or any severe trauma-type patients in this hospital's ER. They send those patients to another hospital because they are not equipped to handle them. I was soon to find out that the rest of the hospital functioned in a similar vein as well.

BeeCause You Loved Me

And although it wouldn't have been my first choice, it was the closest hospital to take Rene to.

11

Insanity

One way to define insanity is continually doing the same thing over and over again and expecting different results. Well, if we are describing insanity that way, then the next several weeks were the epitome of insane.

Rene's family—his three sons, brothers, sisters, mother, and others—were notified of his condition, and they all showed up from California. I will not name names here, but let's just say that the dynamic was horrible at best, and at worst, downright emotionally and physically abusive toward me.

BeeCause You Loved Me

Day three in the hospital, I was told by one of Rene's family members, "You do not count. You have only been married to him for four months. *We* are his true family. You are only his wife. Whenever one of his boys comes into the hospital room to be with him, you should leave."

As you can imagine, those comments—and many, many more like them—went over like lead balloons. I was "sleeping" at the hospital in the room with Rene overnight. I had learned from my mother and her experiences with my grandmother that, if at all possible, you do not leave your loved ones in a hospital by themselves, especially if they are really ill. They need someone there to look after their best interest and be their advocate.

If you have ever either been in the hospital or stayed in the hospital with a loved one, then you know there is no such thing as sleeping. First of all, my "bed" was one of those old hospital reclining chairs. I had to press on the footrest when it was extended to keep it from snapping back at me.

Insanity

Secondly, nighttime is when *all* the different clinical disciplines come to do their jobs. The respiratory therapists (these people are typically pretty cool; if you want to know what is going on with your loved one, talk to them!) came to check on his breathing tube and the respiratory machine. The nurses came in to turn and position Rene. And, for some unknown reason, between three and five a.m. is when the night shift nurses like to give patients bed baths. This consists of turning on *all* the lights; getting soap, water, basins, and cloths; changing Rene's hospital gown and the sheets; bathing him and washing his hair; changing bandages, and so forth. Yes, you read right—at three a.m.

As if that is not enough, right around five thirty a.m. or so, just as we both would be getting back to sleep, the vampires would come in. Yes, I did write vampires. These are the people from the "Lab." They come in white coats, carrying these trays holding all kinds of vials and tubes for the collection of blood and other samples. The reason I call them vampires is that almost all of them seem oh so happy, awake, and thrilled to take someone's blood. They walk in the room and turn on the bright lights, saying, "Oh, I am so sorry, but you know, I have to see. You would not want me poking him in the wrong place, would you?" Then they smile their innocent smiles and begin pulling out their needles and their alcohol swabs to prepare the area before they poke their victim, uh, I mean patient.

Seriously, though, I am sure they are very nice people and their job is critically important. What they do allows the doctors to determine what kind of infections, if any, are going on, to get Rene's WBC (White Blood Cell) count, and many other things. But really, did they *have* to come every time we finally got back to sleep?

Now, back to the "family" dynamics. Things were insane at the hospital. Rene was in critical care; however, people did not quite seem to understand the gravity of his condition. They would ignore visiting hours, sometimes having six to nine people in the room with him in Critical Care. Rene was still in a coma, connected to a ventilator, and on a heart and respiratory monitor, and more. He had tubes coming out of his nose, his lower body parts, and his mouth. However, there seemed to be a lack of regard for standard CCU policies that are in place to help ensure the best possible environment for someone in that condition. Practices and policies such as only two people in the room at a time, limited visitors, no visitors after nine at night, were completely ignored by his relatives. The "family" told me that they could do what they wanted; Rene belonged to them.

There was drama. More drama than all the daytime and nighttime soaps combined. And that is not an exaggeration. There was ex-wife drama; a woman that literally could not stand to be in the same room with him previously now all of a sudden wanted to come and sit by his bedside while he was incapacitated. There was more drama with his three sons and daughter-in-law.

Some of the family members were of the opinion that whenever one or more of his sons entered his hospital room, I should leave—even if I had just arrived, because another son or other people had been visiting. There was mother-in-law drama, sister-in-law drama, and overall family dynamics drama that had originated long before I ever knew them, and unfortunately, unless there is a major shift in the family dynamics, will probably continue for many generations to come.

I had never seen so much drama in my life. I have a severe aversion to drama, so, as you can imagine, I was overwhelmed.

I will not belabor the point or recount everything that occurred. Suffice it to say, though, that as I was facing the facts and learning that the love of my life, my soul mate, and the one with whom I shared all our hopes and dreams for the future, had been shattered by a simple bee sting. Yet, that was not all I had to deal with. I had to deal with the dynamics of a family that had its own challenges in love and communication even when there was not a crisis. Now there was one, and I was at the center of it. I put on my flak jacket and protective gear for what I thought would be a short period of time. That is, until the doctors told me Rene's prognosis.

12

Prognosis

Cold, callous, and without regard for my emotions would be a nice way of describing how the neurologist at this hospital conveyed Rene's prognosis to me. Standing in the hallway of the Critical Care Unit after different tests, including an EEG (Electroencephalogram) to measure Rene's brain wave activity, had been done, the neurologist said this to me.

"We have done physical and neurological tests. The result is that your husband will never be a normal, functioning adult again. You will need to decide what you want to do."

Perplexed and dumbfounded I stood there in the hallway, looking at this doctor, trying to comprehend the words I had just heard. There was no way he was telling me this about the love of my life while standing in the hallway outside my husband's Critical Care Unit room.

This wasn't how the movies showed it. The doctors were supposed to gather everyone together in a quiet room stocked with tissues, with chairs and comfortable sofas on which people could collapse if needed from hearing horrific news. Then, in a quiet and somber voice, one doctor would say something like: "I am so sorry, Mrs. Munoz. I have some very disturbing news to tell you about your husband, and that is why I wanted you to have your friends and family here to support you."

Not this, though, not this way. I stood there in disbelief and anger at not only the words that were said, but the coldhearted way in which they were conveyed. The doctor said those horrible words to me as if he were informing me that the supermarket was out of my

Prognosis

favorite bread: "I am afraid that our shipment of bread has not come in yet, and will not be in until tomorrow."

I refused to believe what I was hearing. I told the doctor, "That is what you say, but I am believing in God for a miracle."

His response was, "In all my years of being a neurologist, I have seen one miracle with someone who has such severe brain damage, and only after several years was this person able to talk and say little words again. It just does not happen."

I honestly cannot tell you what happened after that "hallway" conversation. I don't know. I remember my mother being there later, and swarms of people and family showing up at the hospital. I cannot tell you when I called people or who I called.

My heart was telling me to hold on to Rene, hold on to my faith. My mind was spinning in circles. I can tell you that now I was sure this was a very long and bad dream, and I was sure that, at some point soon, I would awaken and vow to never fall asleep again for a very long time.

BeeCause You Loved Me

No one woke me, and no one was going to. This was indeed a nightmare, but it was a living nightmare. This was now our lives. My baby, my sweetheart, the love of my life was lying there, and all I could see was the man I fell in love with. I was *not* going to give up. Not to mention that I am one of the most stubborn people I know, second only to Rene. Quitting, giving up on him, was *not* an option. And so, my quest for a miracle began.

One of Rene's brothers was a jewel. He loved Rene so much; I could see that his heart was broken. He wanted and needed to "fix" his brother. He needed his brother back and whole just as much as I needed my best friend, lover, and husband back.

Everyone was hurting and perplexed. How could a simple bee sting cripple a man, upend a family, and shatter dreams in seconds? Even the doctors were saying that this did not make sense. If it did not make sense to them, how were all of us supposed to get our heads wrapped around it?

Prognosis

In every family, there is one person, one personality that is the tapestry, holding all the other family members together. Rene was that person. He was the "loved" one.

His winning smile, incredible personality, and ability to make anyone feel special made him the center of the family's attention. Rene was from California, and when he returned home to visit, the response from all his relatives was just short of a family reunion. You may have heard the saying, "Kill the fatted calf, the son has returned." Whenever Rene went home, there was always food, laughter, fun, and a party going on.

Everybody loved Rene. What were we going to do now?

13

Decisions

"Mrs. Munoz? Mrs. Munoz," I heard them saying to get my attention as Rene's mother, brother, sisters, sons, and my family sat with all the doctors as we had the "official" family conference.

The hospital wanted to know if I wanted to pull the plug on my husband. When they found out that doing so was not an option, they wanted to do a tracheotomy on him. This is a surgical operation in which an incision is cut through the front of the neck and into the trachea, or windpipe, to allow someone to breathe without having a

Decisions

tube stuck down their throat and being on a breathing machine.

Up until then, Rene had been receiving his nutrients intravenously but had been losing weight. A feeding tube was then put through his nose to go down his throat and into his stomach, to give him what looked like darkened baby formula. But they were telling me that this was a temporary fix, and Rene's condition was going to be permanent. I was being told that he would require an operation to cut a hole in his stomach so that a feeding tube could be placed directly into it. I was being told that Rene was never going to be able to eat again.

Oh, and I was being told that after the surgeries, he would be moved from CCU into what they called the "step-down unit," which did not require as much intensive monitoring as the CCU. And by the way, Mrs. Munoz, when all that is done, and after he goes onto "the floor"—which is a normal medical/surgical unit, also known as Med/Surg—you will have to decide where you want your husband to go.

BeeCause You Loved Me

Where I want my husband to go? I want him to go home with me! But, depending on the surgeries, level of care required, and so on, I was being told that it might not be feasible for me to take Rene home.

Will you sign for this surgery, will you sign for that surgery; we need to change his medications; will you approve this, and will you approve that. Oh, and he will need physical therapy, occupational therapy, and possibly speech therapy. He will continue to need respiratory therapy, be turned every two hours, and much more.

I quickly realized that this—this world of unknown acronyms, medications, procedures, clinical lingo, and the like—was now becoming Rene's world, and therefore mine. At the time, I did not know the difference between occupational and physical therapy, I did not know what "pressure support" was on the ventilator, I did not know about spasticity, autonomic dysreflexia, or anything else. Nevertheless, I was soon to learn. Moreover, I learned that with every one of these things came major decisions.

I promised Rene in our vows and in our wedding song that I would be there for him; that I would be his voice

Decisions

when he could not speak, his strength when he was weak; and I was going to keep those vows I made to him. And it was then that I made it my quest to become an expert about all things pertaining to Rene and the decisions that needed to be made. He could not make them for himself, but I was going to do everything in my power to make sure he got the best possible care, and that I made the best possible decisions for him.

I didn't leave the hospital for six weeks, and I think I walked outside only a few times in those weeks. I quickly learned that as soon as you leave the hospital room, the doctors and specialists come. It is as if they are lurking around the corner, waiting for you to exit, and then they quickly sneak in, check the patient, and slip away—all while you go pee! I swear, it really is a conspiracy, and they probably keep a running tab of how many patients' family members can be avoided because they have left the room. I am just kidding, but some days it did indeed feel that way. So, you learn not to leave, especially when dealing with a case like Rene's, and so many doctors and specialists needing to speak to you regarding his care.

BeeCause You Loved Me

We were blessed that God and the respiratory therapists (RTs) helped me understand that, in spite of what the doctors were saying, Rene did not need a tracheotomy; he did not even need to be intubated (on a breathing tube). The doctors and I fought over this, but what they did not know is that in those wee hours of the morning, I was learning from everyone—the nurses, the RTs, and all the other disciplines. It's amazing what people will tell you at three o'clock in the morning, and how candid they are about what they know. People always want to share their knowledge, especially that pertaining to their profession.

It's a long story that really involves how some hospitals pressure people into procedures that are not needed in order to make a profit. Let's just say that I had private, full-paying health insurance with no maximum, and that is the insurance which also covered Rene. When they saw me, they saw dollar signs.

I only know this because, as a software techie and previous database engineer, I used to work for a health insurance company and completely understood the billing practices. My insurance was a PPO plan, which hospitals and doctors love, especially when there is no lifetime maximum per individual on costs. Yeah, I know it sounds cynical, but trust me. I had way too many other things to consider and ponder without going down conspiracy lane. That is, until certain conditions and conversations made it quite clear to me what was going on.

Suffice it to say, Rene was extubated and was just fine. He did not need a tracheotomy, and therefore would not be limited to one of only two public facilities (nursing homes) that would take someone with a trache—one of which was owned by the same entity that owned this hospital. I will leave my explanation at that and allow you to draw your own conclusion.

It is unnerving what immediately begins to happen to the human body when it is immobile. All kinds of issues occur. Rene had to be put on many different medications: Heparin to prevent blood clots, Propranolol for blood pressure, medications for seizures and vomiting—over twenty-two medications in all. He also had to be turned every two hours, positioned correctly so that he would not vomit or get more bedsores—and that was just the beginning.

Rene went to the "step-down unit" and eventually onto the Med/Surg floor, where he remained until the middle of November. This meant that we spent Rene's birthday, November 6—his first as my husband—with him in the hospital.

I am not one who easily gives in to circumstances, so I set up a party for my baby. The nurses moved us to the biggest room on the floor to accommodate all the visitors. We decorated his room with streamers, balloons, and party favors. And I invited all our friends and family that were in town to come and help us celebrate. He was still alive, and I was going to celebrate his life!

We got Rene up in a special wheelchair called a cardio or Cadillac chair to support him, and threw him a huge birthday party. For the first time since his accident and waking up from the coma, Rene exhibited emotion.

Decisions

He looked around the room and at the people, at his sons, and then at me, and he began to cry. He knew it was his birthday and that we still loved him. He also knew that he was in a condition he did not want to be in. He turned forty-six that year, in the hospital.

And all during the party, in the back of my mind, I was dreading what was to come. We were soon to leave the familiarity of the hospital's rhythm, however challenging, to go out into the world of long-term care facilities. I knew that the next day I had to go look at nursing homes. At the time, I thought Rene's stay would be short-lived. I thought he would be discharged to a facility, get some more intense therapy, and I would be able to take him home. That was my goal!

But I had found out that, when it was time for him to leave the hospital, my health insurance would not cover home health care, and medical insurance (although most has a home health clause) would not cover what it would cost for me to have twenty-four-hour care for him. I could not lift and turn him by myself, and I needed staff to care for him when I was working. I was going to have to go back to work. I was now incurring significant medical bills, and although I had insurance, the weeks in Critical Care and other things just kept costs climbing. Having lost his income, I was now a single-income mother taking care of two young teenagers and paying for a home that had been purchased based on a two-income family.

But first, I had to go through the laborious and confusing process of trying to find a place to take care of the love of my life. I had to learn how to read yearly state reports, understand infractions and severities, and know what they meant. Clarify staffing ratios for patients, not just during the day, but also on the graveyard shift.

What did the facility look like? How did the patients look? Was the staff friendly? Was the place clean? Were there a lot of unanswered call lights? Did the staff seem harried, frustrated, or unskilled?

There were many more points of consideration, all of which seemed overwhelming. Why couldn't someone just tell me which facility in close proximity to where I lived or worked was the best? Because the hospital "can't." The

Decisions

social workers are not allowed to recommend any particular place; they can only give you a list of all the facilities in your area that have the different disciplines and specialties you or your loved ones need.

So the next day, I was off to visit facilities, review them, and somehow make a decision on where I was going to take my baby. At some point, I would have to make a decision.

14

Facilities

Calling the task of finding a facility that will adequately take care of your loved one "challenging" is an understatement. It is a world of the unknown. It was a whole new world with which I quickly had to become familiar. I had to learn how to navigate through unfamiliar territory, quickly comprehend the overall language, discern the dialects from facility to facility, and create an entirely new space in my brain to retain medical and facility information.

I found out several things. One is that social services in most hospitals are not very social and the services they

Facilities

provide can be somewhat limited. They will point you to resources and websites; however, even though they know the best of the best and the worst of the worst about the facilities in the area, they are not permitted to recommend any. You have to investigate, interview, visit, and come to the determination on your own. As if somehow you have stepped into a world where you have been provided with and read a manual on anterior lobe brain surgery, asked a few questions, and are now ready to perform the procedure yourself. I do not think so.

I quickly learned that Rene's level of care was considered "high acuity." Translated to normal English, it meant that Rene required more attention and time for his care than most facilities wanted to have to provide.

Rene required turning every two hours. His mouth had to be cleaned every two hours. He needed to be shaved, bathed, and cleaned every time he had a bowel movement (which at times was very frequent because of infections he was fighting). He was considered a "total care" patient. And, although the insurance premiums facilities receive are higher for total care patients, there is a numbers game that they play as well.

It is really quite a simple formula by which most facilities operate. They have their income from various sources: health insurance, state insurance (Medicaid), federal insurance (Medicare), and private pay (payment from individuals or their families). Those sources provide all their accounts receivable and gross income for the business on a monthly basis. On the other side, they have expenses such as rent/mortgage, utilities, benefits, supplier fees, etc. However, their largest expense by and large is for employing staff to care for the residents. Facilities have to pay employees and pay their benefits, and unless the staff is in management, they are hourly positions that require overtime compensation when working more than forty hours in a week is required.

How do they make money? Good question, and an easy one to answer. If they can fill the beds in their facility with lower acuity patients—people that require the least amount of staff interaction and care—then they can reduce the amount of staff on certain shifts, but the

Facilities

patients are still charged the same fee. The financial result? More profit. Income remains the same, cost of staffing is down, and it yields a higher net income on the facility's balance sheet.

Are they supposed to accept or reject patients based on this? If the delicate balance of staff and patient acuity is even slightly off or miscalculated, the results for the residents can be devastating, and sometimes even fatal.

Rene's brother, Steve, and I looked at some facilities that had better state reports than others and we finally settled on one located on Mercer Island.

The transition to a facility from a hospital was downright flabbergasting. Instead of a nurse or nurse's aide having no more than four patients, the nurse-to-patient ratio was more like one nurse to every twenty-two or so residents. The aides typically had anywhere from nine to fifteen residents to care for.

And in most care facilities, the distribution of work changes significantly. In hospitals, nurses are primarily responsible for the care of a patient, including all the grooming aspects. The nurses turn, clean, bathe, and monitor the patients on top of providing medical attention such as changing IVs, feeding tubes, dressings, and nutritional management. In hospitals, the aides take vitals and assist the nurses, but are not the primary person that cares for the patients.

Please be forewarned: this is not the case in care facilities. In most, nurses are responsible for dressing changes and management of IVs and feeding tubes. Their major responsibility is dispensing medications. Most of the time their patient load is twenty-plus people, and double that on the late-night shift. Nurses do not have the time or mental bandwidth to provide individual care to the patients, even ones that are total care and require more specialized interaction.

So, who does perform most of the care duties of turning, cleaning, grooming, showering, observing the patients/residents for distress, and overall care? The nursing aides. They are people who have received three months of training and are now the people who primarily interact with and care for the residents. The only things

Facilities

they do not do are hand out medications, deal with IV tubes, or change dressings. Everything else is on the aide.

This was in stark contrast to the hospital and was extremely disconcerting. Most of the aides were overwhelmed. They had to bathe, turn, clean, at at time hand feed patients. They put patients in wheelchairs and took them to therapy. They provided grooming, such as shaving, washing hair, showers, etc. Usually, this was for nine or more patients, and not just within an eight-hour shift, but within a certain time frame for breakfast, another time frame for lunch, and also one for dinner.

I was dumbfounded, to say the least, and it became apparent to me on the first day that Rene was not going to get the attention he needed. It was just not possible. Things like people pulling the curtain so you could not see him would happen. No big deal, right? Wrong. In this facility, Rene's bed was closest to the window, so if the curtain was pulled, one could see into the room, but not see him. He was no longer on heart monitors or any other kind of continuous monitoring, so if something was wrong

BeeCause You Loved Me

with him, hours could go by without anyone noticing, because no one would be going over to the other side of the curtain to check on him.

Therefore, I stayed. I stayed somewhere between sixteen to eighteen hours every day with him. I helped turn him, care for him, and shave him. I made sure they got him bathed, cleaned, clothed, and up into his wheelchair every day, as the doctor had ordered. I wheeled him around the facility, took him to the big TV room to watch TV, and pushed him around the halls. I wanted him to have stimulation and be seen as a person, not just a body in a bed.

Rene's stay at that facility was a short-lived one, however, since he almost coded and we had to call the medics. This time when he was taken to the hospital, I was there, and I got to choose where he went.

This time he went to the number-three hospital in the country, which is located right here in Washington State and is a teaching hospital. This is the place I had originally wanted him to go right after the accident. If he was going to get help anywhere, it was going to be there.

15

Infections

I thought what happened next would only be for a few days, but it literally turned into months. Rene had all kinds of infections in his system and the doctors needed to find out what was causing them.

After a battery of tests—urine samples, blood cultures, and other assessments—it was determined that Rene had multiple infections raging through his system, and he had become septic, also known as septicemia or septic shock. What did that mean? It meant that if they were unable to get the infections under control, bacteria from an infected area of the body could enter his bloodstream. Once there, the bacteria would multiply rapidly, spreading toxins throughout Rene's circulatory system. If left untreated, septic shock, or sepsis syndrome, could ensue, a potentially fatal condition characterized by a dramatic drop in blood pressure and damage to (or failure of) various organs, particularly the kidneys, heart, and lungs.

In laymen's terms, if the infections were not brought under control quickly, Rene could die. You are probably thinking: Then just give him some antibiotics and make it all go away. It is not as easy as you might think.

You see, not all bacteria are vulnerable to all antibiotics. Certain types of bugs or bacteria can only be "attacked" by certain types of antibiotics. And in order to determine which bugs were raging within Rene's system, they had to do urine sample testing as well as a blood culture. The results of those tests in the first twenty-four hours indicate if there is an infection. However, it can take another twenty-four to forty-eight hours to find out the type and sensitivity of the bacteria. And, until that

Infections

specified result comes back, one can only hope that the general broader-based antibiotics, which they were giving Rene, were working to fight the bacteria.

The other tricky element to this dilemma and Rene's medical condition was that he was also allergic to penicillin. This allergy, or a potential allergic reaction to penicillin or any penicillin-based antibiotics, greatly narrowed the field of antibiotics from which they could choose. Sound complicated? That was only the beginning of what I would soon learn had become a more and more complex medical problem for Rene, and sometimes he experienced downright medical mysteries which left some of the best doctors in the country scratching their heads in perplexity.

We learned that Rene had a Urinary Tract Infection (UTI), something not uncommon for people who had indwelling (inserted through the urethra) catheters. He also had aspiration pneumonia from the sputum he was unable to swallow correctly, which ended up in his lungs.

BeeCause You Loved Me

And he had something called Clostridium difficile, which is often referred to as C-diff or C. difficile. This particular bacterium is known to frequent hospitals and is particularly challenging for several reasons. One is that it oftentimes appears when someone is on a course of antibiotics to fight other infections. Unfortunately, the very antibiotics used to kill the bacteria that were causing a UTI or pneumonia also destroy the good bacteria. When someone takes an antibiotic to treat an infection, it often destroys beneficial bacteria as well as the bacteria that are causing the illness. Without enough healthy bacteria, dangerous pathogens such as C. difficile would quickly grow out of control. Thus, Rene was left with yet another infection to fight, and this particular one was easy to catch, but very, very difficult to cure.

What I initially thought would be a "sprint" stay in the hospital ended up turning into a marathon. Rene was very ill, and we were going to be there for a while.

16

Holidays

Needless to say, our first Thanksgiving was a far cry from any way I could have envisioned it. I didn't think I would have believed it if someone had literally shown me a video of the future depicting our first holiday season as a married couple.

Thanksgiving was upon us, and along with it came some difficult challenges that I never thought our family would have to face. We ended up spending not only that Thanksgiving, but also Christmas and New Year's, and starting 2005 with Rene still in the hospital.

BeeCause You Loved Me

I could not bear the thought of Rene spending the Thanksgiving holiday alone and sick. So, I sent my children to my mother's house and I stayed at the hospital with him. His parents were in town, as well as all three of his boys and his daughter-in-law. However, his mother and father were the ones who came and stayed at the hospital that day.

My mother knew I probably would not eat that day if she didn't do something, so she sent my oldest brother to the hospital with food for me and Rene's parents. We enjoyed turkey, corn bread dressing, candied yams, potato salad, fruit salad, and more.

I sat with him, helped turn him, cleaned him, talked to him, and kissed him. He was still my love, and I wanted him to know that no matter what, I loved him with all my heart. And, because Christmas was his favorite time of year, I turned on the Christian radio station, which as of Thanksgiving calls itself the "Christmas Radio Station," so that he could hear Christmas music. I swear, if everyone else in the world wouldn't have threatened his life, Rene would have listened to Christmas music year-round. He

Holidays

loved it! He was like a little kid in a candy store; he never could get enough of it. So, we kept the radio on the station for him throughout the holidays.

Christmas was tough, regardless of how much I decorated his room. I brought in miniature Christmas trees and put up lights, angels, snowmen, and a nativity scene. It did not eliminate the fact that the love of my life was lying there in bed, immobile, and fighting to stay alive.

During that first holiday season, Rene faced many challenges with infections, bedsores, feeding tube issues, medications, and his dislocated jaw (from the field intubation by the medics the day of the bee sting).

To be honest, I did not want hear Merry Christmas, Happy New Year, or any phrase which represented joy or happiness with life. My sweetheart was miserable and suffering, and the only thing I wanted was for our lives to go back to normal.

It took everything I had in me that year to put up a Christmas tree at home. I only did it for the kids, because I knew they wanted one. It was so very difficult. My dear friends Terry and Kit came over to help us decorate, and at one point, I had to leave the room because I came across an ornament Rene had given me the previous Christmas.

I could not figure out how I was supposed to do this without him, but I knew that I had to for my children. I also knew that Rene would want me to do whatever I could to make their holiday happy, so I did my best. You would have to ask them whether or not I succeeded.

The holidays passed, and it was not until the middle of January that Rene was released from the hospital to go to a facility. This in and of itself was another new paradigm to which we would have to quickly become accustomed.

17

Denial

Have you ever been asleep, having a nightmare or a very bad dream, and tried to wake yourself up, but it was difficult? One of those dreams where your conscious mind knows that what your subconscious is experiencing is not real, so it struggles to regain control and awaken you?

I found myself experiencing that very phenomenon; however, the unfortunate thing was that I was not dreaming. There were times I was in the facility, helping turn and clean Rene, and I would need to go get more supplies like Toothettes to clean his mouth, spray for his bottom, or something else. And as I walked down the hall to the supply room, I passed elderly people in wheelchairs talking to themselves, looking into space, crying, or having a conversation with their imaginary friend. I thought, *I am not supposed to be here. I am not supposed to be living this life for another fifty years.* I had just turned thirty-five a couple of weeks before Rene's accident, and it seemed surreal to be spending day in and day out in a place where people either voluntarily go or, more often than not, are sent to finish the final journey of their lives.

One Friday evening it was karaoke night, which was the general entertainment for the predominately elderly population there. The activities director asked me if I wanted to bring Rene down, and I thought, *Why not? There is nothing better to do, and we can get Rene up in his wheelchair and give him a change of scenery.* In those early months, oftentimes he would be more alert and could handle being in his wheelchair longer before he tired.

Denial

As I stood there next to Rene's wheelchair, making sure his head did not fall to one side and wiping the drool from his mouth, the reality of the situation hit me.

I was thirty-five years old, standing in a nursing home next to my forty-six-year-old husband, with a white cloth in my hand to wipe drool from his mouth, listening to really bad karaoke and trying to pretend as if I am enjoying this. How did I get here? How did *we* get here? We should have been going out to dinner, enjoying life, being with friends and family, or having movie night with my kids. We were supposed to be checking items off our "firsts" list; ballroom dancing, going to Paris, going to Jamaica, and so many other wonderful things. We were *not* supposed to be here. We were *not* supposed to be living this nightmare. Our lives, our destinies were not supposed to include the life I now saw before me.

My eyes began to fill with tears, which I quickly wiped away before anyone, especially Rene, could see. And then I looked down at him, in his wheelchair, looking at the people and listening to what was going on, and my heart melted. This was my sweetheart, and *he* was suffering. He was stuck, trapped in that body, and who was I to feel sorry for myself?

I leaned down, kissed him on his precious cheek, and decided that I would sing a song for him that night. And so I did. I sang into the poor quality microphone, with what seemed to be a half-comatose and half-deaf audience looking on, and thought, *If this is where my love is, it is where my heart is, and this is where I will be. It is what it is, and I love that man.*

But loving him did not make everything OK. Loving him did not erase the feeling that we both had been cheated. Loving him did not change the diagnosis, did not change our world. Nor did it make it any easier to accept our new reality. As a matter of fact, loving him made it that much more difficult to accept. I was still in denial.

18

Adapting

No matter what, the one thing that I wanted Rene to know above all else was that he was loved. The only thing

I could imagine that was worse than being trapped in your own body—unable to move, speak, scratch yourself when you have an itch, convey to someone when you're in pain, ask someone to adjust the pillow for you because you are

uncomfortable, eat a meal, or taste food again—was to be in that condition and not feel like anyone loved you.

So I made sure—every day—that Rene knew he was loved, adored, and cherished, and that he meant something to all of us. That was one thing. But oh, there was so much more.

Let me take some time here now to focus on the impact on my children. If I did not, I would truly be remiss, as they are the unsung heroes of this real-life story. Never, not in all my years, have I seen so much courage, strength, love, selflessness, and determination from thirteen- and fifteen-year-old children.

Tyeshia, my fifteen-year-old, had just started her first year (first month, actually) of high school when all this happened. This was the time in her life when it was supposed to be about her! Finding herself, changing and growing from that awkward teenager stage into a young adult. It was time for PSATs, college visits, reviews, and much more. She had just received her learner's permit and started driver's education so that she could get her license.

Adapting

So many wonderful things were supposed to be going on in her life, and in her brother Joshua's life, but instead, their entire world had been turned upside down. Their stepfather, whom they loved and was the only father figure in their lives, had been snatched away and replaced with what I called a "footprint" of him. The reason I say a footprint is that there were still core parts of Rene that he managed to convey. He still smiled, still showed his stubborn streak when he did not want physical therapy, or refused to open his eyes when he was annoyed that a doctor was trying to open them to shine a light in them while he was sleeping. Somehow, Rene still had the ability to convey his personality and make us all laugh and cry with him. He had little ways of letting us know that he was still in there. We had a footprint.

For my children, what was previously just their mother was now a full-time caretaker and advocate for Rene, in addition to working a full-time, sixty-plus-hours-a-week executive job. Only recently have they begun to share with me the totality of the impact on their lives.

BeeCause You Loved Me

Joshua had just joined his junior high football team. He was in those really awkward years before you get to high school and start defining who you are. It was a time in his life when he needed Rene more than ever. He and Rene had bonded and worked out, lifted weights, and done things together. And Rene would help both Tyeshia and Joshua with their homework. They were used to having Rene around.

In those first few weeks of school, it was not uncommon to find us all in the office; the kids at a table or sitting on the floor reading, and Rene and I at the two desks, helping them with their homework. Rene was excellent at math, so the kids quickly learned that he could help them with their math homework much better than I could.

We were a family.

I tried my best to make their lives as normal as possible, but how can you create normalcy out of insanity? We created routines, but they were anything but normal. My children spent Sunday afternoons after church at the facility with Rene and me—not because I

Adapting

made them, or even asked them to, but because they wanted to be there.

They would bring their backpacks, the family laptop, books, and everything they needed to do their homework there. But they also sat with Rene and me, sometimes for hours. They insisted that we continue to have our family movie nights, and the only way we could do that was with Rene. So, unless it was football season—because then it turned into Seattle Seahawks time—we would watch a movie with Rene.

Sitting there in the small room, the curtain pulled for privacy from his roommate, with three chairs cramped around Rene's bed, surrounding him, we would put a DVD in the player and watch. To the end, almost without fail.

You can say or think what you want, but Rene knew and understood what we were doing. I say that because no matter what, he would make sure he stayed awake until the credits were rolling on the screen. I would often see him focused on keeping his eyes open, since some of the medications and his condition itself caused him to be very tired at times, to make sure he watched the movie with us.

It was our "family time," and for as much as we could get out of it, it was one of the few things we had left that even resembled our old lives. Sitting on folding chairs in a care facility, watching a movie with the man we loved.

And, my children were there every Sunday, without fail. There were times when they were tired and had homework to do or tests to study for, but they let me know that for them, not being there was just not an option.

They would talk to Rene, kiss him, make him smile, and even pick on him. If he was not feeling well, which sometimes could make things pretty difficult, they would comfort him.

And that was just part of it. Oftentimes, I would come home to a meal—yes, cooked by my children—or the house had been cleaned up and other things done. They tried so much to lighten my load any way they could. A

Adapting

load no child should ever have to bear, but due to different catastrophic situations, often do.

Recognizing that I did not want their youth to be robbed from them, I made a promise to myself that they would enjoy their teenage years. And as I was able to show them that I was OK, I began to push them little by little out into the world of their teenage friends.

Movies, birthday parties, sleepovers, and traveling the world became part of their teenage experience. One only gets to be a teenager once, and I wanted to make sure they didn't miss it. Yes, their teenage years would be different, but it did not mean that these would have to be missed altogether.

I was blessed that they were able to travel to many places before either of them turned eighteen. To Japan, Mexico, India, Paris, Greece, Italy, Washington, DC, and others while on mission and Student Ambassador trips. So along with this tragedy, they were also able to see the world, and be seen by the world for the incredible people they both are.

BeeCause You Loved Me

My babies. I love them dearly, and I am truly blessed that God granted me such beautiful and precious gifts.

After the accident, trying to adapt to my whole family never being at home together, not being able to be with all the people I loved at the same time, was excruciating for me. As I hoped and prayed for a miracle, it was not uncommon to hear me say, "I can't wait until I can go home and my whole family will be there. I can't wait until I go straight home from work, and Rene and the kids will all be there. I can't wait until we can all have dinner together again. I can't wait until..."

19

Waves

Sometimes they are small. Sometimes they are large. Sometimes you see them coming. Sometimes you do not. Sometimes they come with gale-force winds; sometimes they drown you like a hurricane. And sometimes, they are downright tsunamis. They come from nowhere, suck you under, and you wonder if you will ever gulp fresh air or see dry land again—and sometimes you pray to God that you don't.

What am I talking about? What are these "waves" that show up on nice days or rainy days, while you are

BeeCause You Loved Me

driving or in a grocery store, while you are watching a movie or in the middle of a presentation at work?

They are the torrential emotional cycles that overcome me, often when I least expect it. The floodgates open; emotions that I have been so proud of managing in the midst of all this insanity sometimes choose to unleash themselves; they break through the barriers I have built to keep them in and are released in a tide that sometimes feels like it is going to take me under.

I will never forget the first "wave" of emotions that hit me. It was about six weeks into Rene's ordeal and I was with my two children in a grocery store near our home. It was the first shopping trip I had been on since everything happened.

People had been very generous in buying or bringing us food, so I had not had to go shopping. We were in a grocery store in Redmond, and it was around eight in the evening. The kids and I had split up to "divide and conquer" so we could get in and out of the store quickly.

Waves

I was walking down one of the main aisles at the back of the store, on my way to get milk, when I passed an end cap—you know, the end of the aisle where they put products that are on sale (in this case it was a refrigerated one). I looked at it and it contained coffee creamers of different flavors on sale, and as I mentioned before, Rene was a coffee lover. So I thought, *Oh, I will pick up a couple of different ones for Rene. He will like these flavors.*

I reached up to grab the creamer, and the tsunami hit me. I felt sick to my stomach, and I almost passed out because I realized that Rene might not *ever* be able to drink coffee again, let alone add flavored creamer to it. I realized that I may never be able to shop for food for him again; he may never be able to eat a meal I have prepared for him. He was on a feeding tube attached to a hole in his stomach, and nothing went in but feeding tube formula, which is much like baby formula but with more nutrients, protein, and fiber.

At that moment, I felt like I was going to die. Literally. The room began to spin, and I thought, *Oh no, I cannot scare my kids like this. Pull yourself together, Monique, pull yourself together.* So I did, enough to get the kids, and say, "You know what? I am not feeling so well. Let's get checked out."

It was one of many "waves" that would hit me over time. Not all were tsunamis like that one, but that first wave was part of my initial realization that our lives would never be the same.

They do not come as frequently now as they did in the early days, and I have learned how to ride most of them out without requiring emotional resuscitation, but they still come. And, just when I think I have learned to ride them out, one sneaks up on me in a way I did not expect, ensuring that I never lose touch with my new reality.

Waves.

20

Changes

My life and the lives of my children had changed. We were no longer the happy family of four living in a beautiful home east of Seattle and experiencing normal day-to-day life. We had experienced a paradigm shift.

The kids were young when this happened. Tyeshia was fifteen years old and had just started high school, and Joshua was thirteen and in junior high.

It was either change and adapt or...hmmm...or what? Crawl under a rock, live in denial and fall apart? The alternative was not a choice, so we changed.

BeeCause You Loved Me

Hospital emergency rooms, care facilities, tube feedings, and the smell of urine and bowel movements.

Life as we knew it changed from focusing on being at home and starting a new family life together to me figuring out how I could fit in a concert, a football game, and the emergency room all in the same night. My children went from family dinners with four to oftentimes the two of them eating alone with each other.

There were so many things that shifted in our lives, so many things that changed, but there were two things that did not—our love for each other and our love for Rene—unless you count our growing to love and appreciate each other more as a change.

Our love and commitment was only accomplished by God's grace and mercy, and by the incredible friends and family He surrounded us with for support.

21

Support

I've decided that the mere mentioning of friends throughout this book would not accurately convey the profound impact some very special people had on my life. So I have dedicated a chapter to them, because to do less would just seem wrong.

I have been truly blessed with people in my life; women and men whom I call my "heart friends." Most of these people have known me for many years, and have seen me through different phases and periods in my life. Some, however, came along just before or during the time of the accident and ongoing tragedy in my life, and have stuck by my side. No matter when these individuals entered my life, they are truly dear to me, and I am humbled and blessed to call them friends.

These "heart friends" are the people that dropped everything they were doing on a Saturday evening to come to the hospital and spend Rene's forty-fifth birthday with us. They are the people that loved me enough—no matter how much I protested, and no matter how difficult it was for me—to make me leave the hospital, get away briefly, and go have a meal with them. They are also the people that for the first several weeks, when I could not bear to leave Rene's side, brought food to me. They picked up my children, brought them home, stayed with them and made sure they were fed. My dear friends are the ones that called me in the morning, checked on me at night, and sat with me during the wee hours in the hospital.

These people have seen my tears, cried with me, had their hearts broken with me, challenged me to live, loved me enough to understand when I could not bring myself

Support

to do any more than just sit by Rene's bedside, and cared enough to nudge me to continue trying to live my life.

My dear sweet friends loved me, cared for me, allowed me to confide in them. They would talk to me on the phone late at night, when I was driving home from the hospital or Rene's facility, to make sure I was OK and didn't fall asleep at the wheel from exhaustion. These people prayed with me, and prayed for me. They called their family, friends, and friends of friends to ask that they pray for Rene, me, and the kids, and to have their church congregations pray for us.

They are the people who came rushing to the hospital when Rene's family members physically attacked me. They are the people who would come with me the few times I went out to dinner, when I would inevitably receive a phone call that something was wrong with Rene and he was being rushed to the hospital.

These are the people who saw me at my ugliest moments, my most difficult times, the most horrible events in my life, and they still love me. These people not only chose to love me; they chose, in all their different ways, to stand by my side. And for that, I am forever grateful.

I learned that many people can come in and out of a person's life, and that most will not be the "one" type of friend you need. If you look, you will see that each person God sends into your life brings something special to you and/or draws something special out of you. I learned that there are many different types of people in the world, but there are only a few I can call "heart friends."

To those people, and you know who you are, I am eternally grateful. All of you are just as much a part of this story as Rene, my kids, and I. You are the tapestry which held our lives together when we were incapable of doing it ourselves.

My prayer is that others will be as blessed and as honored as I have been to have very special people like this come into their lives, for whatever duration ordained, because it deeply enriches your being, strengthens your spirit, and enlightens your soul.

22

Choices

Rene's condition required a copious amount of choices regarding his care. There were so many different choices to be made on any given day, that it could drive a person insane.

Should we put in a Baclofen pump to help reduce the spasticity in his arms and legs to prevent them from getting so stiff (which is also very painful for him)? Should I change his PEG tube to a G/J tube because he is vomiting his formula? Should we change his blood thinner from Heparin to Coumadin? Would it be better for Rene to have a surgically placed subcutaneous catheter instead of an indwelling Foley catheter (to empty the urine from his bladder into a bag), because the facility caregivers kept inadvertently pulling out his catheter when they turned him, causing internal damage, severe bleeding, and pain to his urethra? Should we change his tube feeding rate to increase his caloric and fiber intake to assist in healing his decubitus ulcers (bedsores)? But if we do, will his stomach be able to absorb the additional formula, or will he have an episode of emesis (vomiting) because he can't hold it in? And, if that were to happen, then he could aspirate (the vomit could go into his lungs) and he could get aspiration pneumonia—or worse yet, asphyxiate, because his lungs would fill up and he would not be able to breathe, and he could die.

So many choices. And, if I made the wrong one, it could prove to be deadly for him.

There were two dumbfounding things about making all these choices. One, I had to make them all alone. His family and I were estranged, and even when we were talking, if they asked how Rene was doing and I went into

Choices

all the medical details, they would not-so-politely say, "You know, we really don't need all those details, just tell us the basics."

And two, I really do mean I was making them alone. The doctors in the facility and in the hospitals could only give me options. Even they did not have the "whole" picture of Rene. I was the only constant person in his life on the "caregiving team" for Rene. I was the one that noticed if he looked just a little different from one day, or even minute, to the next. I was the one that remembered to tell the doctors that he had to have a certain type of antibiotic prophylactically before starting any other antibiotics to prevent C-diff. It was I that would inquire about alternative and proactive treatments, their feasibility, and how they might possibly help Rene.

Amazingly enough, it was more than a year after the accident occurred that I found out the name of the state Rene was in: Minimally Conscious State (MCS). A step above persistent vegetative state. He was able to kind of smile at me, follow me, pucker for kisses, and look at me with those big, beautiful brown eyes of his. He would watch TV, and go through normal sleep and wake cycles, but I could not tell if he responded to me sometimes because he knew I was his wife, or because I was the one that kept him safe and comforted him if he was in pain or scared.

When the head of neurological rehab at the second hospital diagnosed Rene with MCS, she said to me, "I don't know if this makes it easier or harder, but he is not in PVS. He can hear, respond to stimuli, and understand some things."

Well, at the time I was thinking that it made it easier, because I still had a "footprint" of my sweetheart left, and as long as I had that, I had hope that I would get the whole him back. And even in the midst of that statement by the doctor, I saw two things in her eyes as she looked at me: empathy for my pain, and the question, *What are you going to do?* There were enough choices to be made to drive any human being out of his or her mind, or at least curl up on the floor in the fetal position, thumb in

Choices

mouth. And trust me, there were times I thought about doing just that!

Thankfully, God's grace was so sufficient for me, and His mercies truly did renew every morning. Writing this book, looking back and realizing the magnitude of the weight that was on me, it now brings tears to my eyes as I realize just how much grace God gave me, because although sometimes seemingly daunting, never once did I feel overwhelmed by a decision. I always had a "sense" that I knew what was right, and God truly blessed me to understand Rene's medical condition and all the medicines, issues, and circumstances around it so that I could make sure I took care of my sweetheart.

Sometimes, the choices were as simple as working with his care team to figure out what kind of air mattress he needed so that his pressure ulcers (bedsores) would not get worse and would begin to heal. Other times, the choices laid before me were akin to a large buffet table with all kinds of food spread in front of a very hungry person, but the option to choose only one.

BeeCause You Loved Me

Through the midst of it all—and I do mean *all*—God was and is so faithful.

23

Reality

I slept only on my side of the bed, on my left side, facing the door. It was the same position I was in when Rene was well, there, and spooning me to sleep every night. I could not bring myself to sleep on Rene's side of the bed or on his pillow. I did not even want to. What I wanted was to have my sweetheart there in bed with me. I wanted to feel the warmth of his body next to mine. I wanted to feel him kiss my cheek and neck. I wanted to hear him whisper "I love you" in my ear, and I wanted to wake up and find him still there in the morning.

BeeCause You Loved Me

However, the reality was that the nights when I wasn't staying at the hospital or at the facility with him, I was at home, in our bed, alone. And, I found that I did not, could not, sleep the same. In Rene's arms, I had begun to find the best sleep I had ever experienced in my life. In Rene's arms, I knew he loved me, and I felt safe.

Every time I walked into our bedroom, it reminded me that Rene was not there. We had just moved into the house when we got married. It was not my room; it was ours, Rene's and mine. But Rene was not there and had not been for almost two years now.

My life had changed so much from what I thought it would be. I was now a single parent and caregiver to a completely disabled husband. Life was different, and I realized it was not going to change for the better anytime soon.

After two years and three sets of holidays, it never got easier trying to figure out how to balance my commitment to Rene and not make my teenagers, as gracious and selfless as they were, have to spend Christmas in a care facility.

Reality

So many things were different from what I had imagined.

24

2007

Days turned into weeks, weeks turned into months, and believe it or not, months turned into years. And, during this time, there were countless calls in the wee hours of the morning to my cell phone from the facility, telling me that there was something wrong with Rene. We made over one hundred visits to hospital emergency rooms and saw countless neurologists, urologists, diagnostic radiologists, rehab specialists, dentists, surgeons, hospitalists, and internal medicine doctors, to name a few. There were physical therapists, occupational therapists, speech therapists, wound care nurses and specialists, wound clinics, otolaryngologists, ER doctors and nurses, X-ray technicians, radiologists, medical assistants, nursing aides, nutritionists, durable medical equipment representatives, facility directors, charge nurses, unit nurses, janitors, and the like that, unfortunately, Rene and I came to know very well.

All in all, there were too many visits and too many close calls. I slept with my cell phone on; actually, it was *never* off, unless I was on an airplane. I called it my "bat phone." It was my personal link to Rene that any doctor, nurse, aide, therapist, or anyone else could reach me on. It was literally our lifeline.

By the time we were getting close to three years of this ongoing, living nightmare, it was obvious that Rene, the kids, and I were all wearing down. Many at the prominent teaching hospital here knew us not only by sight, but also by name. When Rene and I would arrive at the emergency department, we were greeted by some of the staff by name. It was not uncommon to hear, "Hello, Rene, back to see us again so soon?" Or, "Weren't you

BeeCause You Loved Me

just here a couple of days ago?" Or, "Hi, Monique, another late night, huh? What is wrong with Rene this time?" I found it amazing that the gift of love we shared was able to transcend Rene's illness, and we still had a dynamic with people similar to when Rene was well. Everyone knew our names, loved to interact with us, and gave us special attention. But now, instead of restaurants and grocery stores, it was in hospitals and procedure rooms.

I knew where all the bathrooms were, how to get from one main section of the hospital to another, the hours the cafeteria opened and closed, and if the cafeteria was closed, the time and location of the food cart, which offered leftover sandwiches, fruit and cheese trays, chips, and the like. More often than not, if I was able to grab something to eat at all, it was from the cart, so it was critical for me to know when it would stop by the emergency department and other floors during the wee hours of the morning.

Another indicator that this insanity had lasted too long was I knew all Rene's medications, all seven pages of them. I knew the names, how to spell them, how to pronounce them, most of the brand and generic names (they are often very different, and sometimes if it was not caught, Rene would be prescribed a double dose of the same medication), the dosage, how they were to be given, and the frequency (Q2, QID, PRN, etc., all ways the medical field indicates how often a medication should be given).

And finally, the last yet most important indicator that this journey was truly taking its toll was Rene's health. In two and a half years, his feeding tube had been dislodged or pulled out (not by him; he was unable to move his arms or hands) fourteen times. That alone was fourteen visits and about 160 hours in the emergency department. And there was much more. Rene had many, many bouts with aspiration pneumonia from vomiting out the feeding tube, pointing it toward his lungs instead of into his stomach. His bedsores were not healing, and the frequency and severity of his visits continued to increase. One month, he was in and out of the hospital so much that he only spent one continuous twenty-four-hour period at the facility.

And he was tired. I was tired. Tyeshia and Joshua were tired. No, let me correct that—we were beyond fatigued. My mother sometimes says, "My soul *IZ* tired," meaning that the depth of exhaustion and fatigue she feels is beyond the physical, natural, or even emotional; she was worn-out down to her soul.

Well, all our souls were tired, and at the start of 2007, something began to shift. I remember sitting in church on January 2, 2007, and hearing the associate pastor speak the message: "2007, a Perfect Year." It was then, sitting in the seat listening to this message, that God spoke to my heart yet again. But this time, it was a message that shook me to the very core of my spirit. God spoke to my heart and showed me that Rene was not going to be with us in 2008. You see, not only is the number seven God's number to represent perfection, it also represents *completion*. God was letting me know that Rene's journey was going to be completed that year.

I sat there with tears in my eyes, and my spirit pleaded, "Lord, no. Please don't let it be so." And I could feel Him ever so lovingly say to my heart, "It must be."

At that moment, I realized that the miracle I had been hoping and praying for was not the plan God had for us all.

However, true to my slightly stubborn form, I tried to put it out of my mind, convince myself that maybe it was just me, although I knew it wasn't. And it was as if God said, "I know that you are not going to want to accept this, so am I going to help you."

And help me He did. But it was not in the way you would think. God opened my eyes by letting me see Rene's true condition. It was deteriorating. By the second week in January, he had gone to the ER twice, and the second time they admitted him and he was in the hospital for over a week.

He returned to the facility for a few days, and then he was back in the hospital again. And this pattern continued almost every week, and often we were in the ER several times a week. That is, if Rene had not been admitted from the previous visit.

One thing after another continued to go wrong and began to compound issues. The things we had been able to manage and seemingly master over the previous two and a half years were no longer responding to the courses of treatments they used to respond to. The doctors and I ended up scratching our heads and saying, "Hmmm...now this one is new. Rene sure is keeping us on our toes." More antibiotics were required, solutions were more difficult to find, and apparent resolutions lasted for much shorter periods.

So, in late February 2007, as I was driving across the State Route 520 Bridge to meet Rene at the emergency room again for about the twentieth time that year already, I began to cry. Not those little tears that run down your face. I mean sobbing, snorting, gasping for air, uncontrollable bawling—and yes, while I was driving.

I tried calling my family and several friends, but could not reach anyone. It was a Sunday, a rare beautiful February day, and evening was approaching. The water in

2007

Lake Washington was beautiful, the Seattle skyline was as breathtaking as always, and that was where I lost it. Through my weeping, I had the most candid conversation I had ever engaged in with God.

"All right, Lord, I don't know how much longer I can take this. More than that, I don't know how much longer Rene can take this. I have been praying, waiting, hoping, and interceding all this time for your Divine intervention and a miracle for Rene. I WANT MY HUSBAND BACK! But, if for some reason, and it appears that this is the case, it is *not* Your will to heal my husband, then just take him home to be with YOU. He is suffering, we all are suffering, and the *only* reason I have been fighting so hard is because I believed that You would *heal* him. So Lord, You either heal my baby, or you take him home to be with You. But this in-between, this limbo, this suffering has got to end. So, you either heal him or take him home. October will be three years this has been going on. You have until then!"

BeeCause You Loved Me

I can almost hear the gasping of disbelief as I write this. Yes, I did indeed say that to God. Was I being disrespectful? No. I was very plainly doing as the Bible says: "Let your requests be made known unto God." Therefore, I did, very earnestly and very clearly.

What ensued in the following months I can only say was grace. When I finally gave in and realized that I was willing to accept more than just one option, of a miraculous healing for Rene here on earth, things began to change. Not with Rene's health, because we continued going in and out of the hospital, back and forth to emergency departments and the facility. No, things began to change within me.

My spirit and soul began to accept that I might just not "get my way" about this. That although we all had so much faith for Rene's healing, God's thoughts are not our thoughts, and His ways are not our ways. And I do not always understand, but I do trust His will.

Rene and I were both worse for the wear, and the impact of all this began to hit me. Oh, and did I mention that Tyeshia was turning eighteen that spring and graduating from high school? Yes, she was, and at the same time, the kids' grandpa, whom they loved dearly, was diagnosed with stage-four lung cancer.

He was in the hospital and dying. My poor children, there was so much going on. So much to celebrate and mourn at the same time. Death was staring them in their faces with their grandpa, but we were soon to find out that it was also knocking on Rene's door as well.

25

Grief

Rene and I celebrated our third wedding anniversary the same way we had celebrated our first: with him in the condition he was in, and with me bringing extra-large singing balloons, gifts, and having a small party. The only difference was that this year I was unable to take him home like I did the first year, where family and friends celebrated our anniversary with us.

That was quite a celebration. I had gotten Rene in his wheelchair, set up transportation, and planned a party. It was our first wedding anniversary, and my goodness, we were going to celebrate and be surrounded by the people we loved, in our home. It was even more special because it was going to be the first time I was able to take Rene home since the accident on October 12, 2004. Our first wedding anniversary was on May 22, 2005.

For that wonderful occasion, a dear friend of mine, Terry, made a special wheelchair ramp so that I could get Rene from the entertainment room, up the two flights of stairs, and into the rest of the house.

We decorated, my mother cooked food, and I invited our friends and family. One way or another, Rene and I were going to celebrate our love.

When we got Rene home, everyone was already there. He was still very sensitive to noise or being crowded, so I let everyone know to speak softly and that only one or two people at a time should greet him.

Everyone was so happy to see him out of bed and in his wheelchair, and as he looked around and saw all of us there to celebrate our wedding anniversary, he began to cry. This was no small accomplishment for him, as showing and expressing deep emotions took a lot of his energy. But he did. I kissed his face as he wept, kissed away his tears, just like he used to kiss away mine. I told him how much we all loved him, and we both wept.

I wheeled him around the house, to remind him that he still had a home, and that it was my hope that he would return here one day for good.

His desk, and our room, closet, and bathroom, were still the way he had left them the day of the accident. This was our home, and I was waiting for my husband to come back to the kids and me.

Well, fast-forward to May 2007. The party was in his room at the facility, a few days after our anniversary because I had to be out of town on business for the actual day. But nonetheless, we celebrated. I kissed him, he puckered and kissed me back, and then I did something that just sent me over the emotional edge.

We had had our wedding professionally videotaped, and I brought the DVD with me to the facility to play for not only Rene and I, but for the people there that cared for him.

Grief

I put the DVD in. I wanted them to see the man I fell in love with. I wanted them to see our wedding and our love. What I forgot in the midst of wanting them to see this was that Rene and I were both watching it as well.

Oh, how I missed being in his arms! How I missed hearing his voice, feeling his touch, and making love with him to a point where we transcended beyond our emotional and physical connection and entered into a wonderful spiritual experience. I missed him spooning me at night, kissing my face, loving me. I missed hearing his voice, listening to him preach, minister, prophesy, and hearing him laugh. I missed my *husband*.

Seeing us on that screen three years before did something to me. The reality that I only had had four months with him as my husband before the bee sting was just unbearable. I had had four months of us as husband and wife, as a family, before all this happened.

It was just not fair. And I was about to find out that it was only going to get worse.

BeeCause You Loved Me

Sensing this in my spirit, during the summer months I began to have conversations with my children about the will of God. I began preparing them that it very well might be God's that Rene's healing would come on the other side of heaven.

At the same time, God was preparing me. More and more, it became evident that I had put my life on hold for almost three years; that I had not been living, only surviving.

The summer continued on, and I began to take little emotional baby steps toward the realization that I could lose Rene. By this time, I had forgotten about that grief-stricken and tearful prayer I had said so many months before while driving across the SR 520 bridge, but God had not. As a matter of fact, I truly believe that it was on that day that my soul truly cried out for the will of God, instead of my own.

My birthday came and went in September, and I celebrated it with friends and family. I didn't want anything big or a lot of presents, I just wanted to be with the people I loved. I spent time with Rene, time with my family, and time with my friends. Rene had stabilized a little, and I could feel myself beginning to remember what it was like to go beyond just existing, and to actually live.

And then, about a week after my thirty-eighth birthday, God made His will known.

I got a frantic phone call from a nurse at the facility at about two thirty in the morning. He told me that they were not calling the ambulance, they were calling the medics. You may wonder: What is the difference? An ambulance transports someone to the hospital, and may provide oxygen and basic care. Medics, on the other hand, provide life-sustaining care. These are the people who respond when someone is having a heart attack, stroke, etc. They can give some meds, shock people with paddles, assess situations, and get people to the hospital quickly while still working to sustain their life. In Washington State, they are a part of the fire department. They are the people you want to respond if your life is ever in danger, and I was informed that Rene's was.

BeeCause You Loved Me

His oxygen saturation had suddenly dropped to about forty-two. Let's just say that if it is below ninety-two, oxygen is administered to you. In the CCU, if it drops below ninety or ninety-one, alarms go off, nurses come in, and respiratory therapy is typically called. At an O_2 saturation of forty-two, Rene really wasn't breathing.

I threw on the clothes I had picked out for work and went to the hospital. This time, he was too critically ill to take across the water to our normal hospital. The medics took him to the closest hospital, which was about five minutes from the facility.

By the time I got there (I lived twenty-five minutes away), Rene was in the emergency department, as I expected. But then I saw something I did not expect. My baby was in a room with about twelve people buzzing around very rapidly, and he was intubated. He was on life support—on a breathing machine. He had never had to be put back on one since his first admission to the hospital almost three years before.

His big brown eyes with those beautiful eyelashes found me as I walked in. He must have heard my heels

Grief

clicking on the tile floor of the emergency room. He began to gag on the feeding tube, which is not uncommon, but is heartbreaking to see. And at that moment, my heart sank. My baby was suffering so much. He was worse than he had ever been before, and unbeknownst to me, it was worse than I had even realized.

They temporarily stabilized him and rushed him up to the CCU. Rene's vitals were bad; his blood pressure and pulse were dropping because there was an infection in his system that had caused him to become septic. The infection had begun to attack his vital organs, and they were beginning to shut down.

His ER doctor there was literally an angel here on earth. We were so fortunate to have her as his doctor when he was admitted. We got him to the CCU, and because it was morning and she was the overnight doctor, she talked to me briefly and let me know that Rene's condition was very serious, and that the next doctor would be speaking with me soon.

BeeCause You Loved Me

When that doctor came on shift, she introduced us, and then a little while later he called me out of Rene's room to speak with me.

We stood there, outside Rene's CCU room, looking through the glass walls and doors, watching his heart monitor and his vitals, which were not improving, and the doctor said the following words to me that I did not expect to hear.

"Mrs. Muñoz, Rene is very sick, is not breathing well, and has an infection which has now become septic." At this point, I was thinking, *Yeah, yeah, been there, done that*. This wasn't our first trip to the CCU. The doctor continued talking, and that is when I began to understand the gravity of the situation.

"We have given him several drugs to attempt to get his blood pressure and pulse back up, but they have not worked. We are also flooding him with fluids, to attempt to raise his blood pressure, and that is not working either. If he does not respond within several minutes to these drugs, it may mean that the infection has gone too far and Rene's organs have already begun to shut down. Now, we can give him another type of drug that may work, but that in itself could cause other kinds of significant damage."

"Huh?" Not as in I did not understand what he was saying. Analytically and medically, I knew exactly what he was saying. My husband was dying, right then, and possibly this morning he was going to die.

After all this information was provided, the "bomb" question came. "So, Mrs. Muñoz, we know that you have him as a full code, and we can follow your wishes and do everything medically possibly to save him, including using the paddles and pushing some more severe medications which may cause additional damage. Do you still want him to be a full code?"

Oh my God. This was "that" time. You know, the time in the movies we all have watched where the gut-wrenching decision has to be made by the loved one, and we are talking to the screen, trying to convey our opinions to the screenwriters for a script that has already been written, and then are just waiting and watching to see how they decided to end the story.

BeeCause You Loved Me

This was our story, and no one warned me that I was going to have to pen some of the script myself. OK, well, maybe *Someone* did. Do you think that maybe, just maybe, this day is what God was trying to tell me way back on January 2 of the same year? Maybe so.

I stood there, dumbfounded and speechless. I asked the doctor some questions, and asked him to give me a few minutes. Then I prayed; I rang up heaven.

Surprisingly, my answer was this: *If God is trying to take him home, and the medications are not working, then I am not going to interfere with God.* I always told God that if Rene was going to go, He was going to have to take him. What did that mean for Rene? It meant that if he was tired and trying to go home to be with the Lord, I was not going to prolong his misery here on earth.

I went into the room where Rene was, leaned over the bed, and kissed his cheek. He had tubes coming out of almost every orifice of his body. He had a breathing tube in his mouth, going down his throat into his lungs; he had a feeding tube, he had a nasal trumpet in one of his nostrils for suctioning (from the facility), he had a Foley

Grief

catheter for urine, and they had put a tube in his bottom attached to a bag to catch his running diarrhea. Not to mention that he had several IV lines attached to his hands, arm, and foot.

As I kissed him again, he opened those beautiful, loving eyes of his and looked at me. And I began to talk to the love of my life. "Baby, I know that I have been telling you for almost three years that you keep fighting in there and I will keep fighting out here. And you have fought. And all this time, I thought I was fighting for you, but I realize that it has been you fighting for me. To stay here for me. You wanted to make sure that I was OK. And baby, I will keep fighting for you out here as long as you want. I love you with all my heart, and I am here. I love you more today than I did yesterday, and more than the day we got married."

And as I looked into his eyes and caressed his forehead with my hand, I then spoke to him gently, saying, "But if you are tired, it is OK. You have tubes all over, infections raging through your system, and a stage-

BeeCause You Loved Me

four ulcer (bedsore to the bone) that is not healing and has only gotten worse over three years. You have recurring urinary tract infections and have been through so much. If you are tired, it's OK. If you are tired of fighting, it's OK. I will be OK. If you are not, I will fight for you out here as long as you want to fight in there, but I need to let you know that it's OK. I understand, and if your soul *IZ* tired, I understand."

At this point, Rene looked at me and lifted one eyebrow as if to say, *Are you sure you will be OK?*

I looked at him, tears streaming down my face, and replied, "I will be OK, baby. I will be OK. You have given me the greatest gift that anyone could possibly give me. You showed me the Father's love, and in that love, you gave me a safe place to be me. I am what I am because you love me."

And then I began to sing the theme song from our wedding. Because we had both been each other's strength when we were weak, I was his voice when he couldn't speak, and his love had given me a gift I did not know was possible: he gave me, me.

Grief

I would later realize that it was at that point, in the CCU of a hospital in the Eastside area of Seattle, that Rene Muñoz decided it was OK for him to go home to be with the Lord. But before he did, he had some surprises in store for us.

I called my mother; later she said the only reason she knew it was me was because I called her Mom. I told her that Rene was dying. Within an hour, she and my brother were there at the hospital to support me.

But Rene was not quite ready to cross the threshold of death's door. Within a couple of hours, without any further intervention by the doctors, Rene began to get better. His vitals improved, his blood pressure and pulse returned to more acceptable levels, and his skin color got better.

After a few more hours, it looked like Rene was doing a little better still. Well, I will not take you through the next several days, but suffice it to say that I thought the message I was getting from Rene was loud and clear: *I am not ready to go home yet.* So much so that his breathing got better, and we discussed the fact that the next day, Saturday, we would be able to take him off the "vent" and he would be able to just have an oxygen mask.

Well, apparently Rene did not like the idea of waiting, because somehow, using only his tongue, Rene was able to extubate (take the tube out) himself! I guess after about a week of being on the ventilator, he was ready to have that tube out, so he used his tongue to work it loose. Unbelievable! I was thinking, *My baby is fighting! He wants to live!*

Rene got so much better that he could be discharged off the Unit to a regular floor. He stayed there for almost a week, actually having one of our very sweet neighbors who is a respiratory therapist work with him and see him for the first time since his accident. This was two days before the hospital decided to discharge him and he went back to the facility. It was amazing because she works only a few days each month, and usually not on that floor.

He ended up not needing oxygen, and was discharged on Friday, October 12—exactly three years to the day after his accident. Well, maybe I was going to get my miracle after all!

So, I met him at the facility to make sure he got all settled, and that his medications were set up correctly. I made sure that everything was in order, spent a little time with him, and kissed him good-bye. My mother's birthday was the next day, October 13, but I was going out to dinner Friday with her, my brother, and a friend of Mom's to celebrate both their birthdays. I figured I would spend more time with Rene either later that evening or on Saturday, my mother's actual birthday.

But something funny happened after I said good-bye to him and walked down the familiar hallway. I felt this weight about not coming back to the facility at all, almost as if I did not know if I could return.

Well, at 6:14 a.m. on Saturday, October 13, I found out why, but it would be several weeks before I truly understood. That morning, my cell phone rang. It was the same nurse at the facility that had called me when Rene had been critically ill a couple of weeks before. But there was something wrong. The nurse was sobbing. In three years, I had never seen him even tear up. He was sobbing because he was calling to tell me that Rene had died.

"WHAT?!"

October 13, 2007, three years and one day after the simple bee sting, on my mother's birthday, at the age of forty-eight, Rene Arthur Muñoz, the love of my life, quietly slipped away from this earth during the middle of a shift change, to go home to be with the Lord.

My sweetheart was dead. And although I thought I had prepared myself for this, I had no idea of the emotional tsunamis that were headed my way.

No idea whatsoever.

26

Good-bye

Caskets. Cemetery plots. Funeral homes. Eulogies. They are all part of the ritual in American culture we utilize to say good-bye to our loved ones. And they are, in my humble opinion, the most morbid and difficult choices a human has to make.

In what clothes should I bury the love of my life? What shirt, socks, suit, and tie are appropriate to be put in for all eternity? OK, OK, maybe it sounds a little melodramatic, but it is very true, and I hated every moment of it.

BeeCause You Loved Me

On top of it all, I had changed jobs and the life insurance coverage that I had on myself and Rene was supposed to be continued with my COBRA. However, my previous company did not put it in. Therefore, I did not have insurance, and was only ten days away from the life insurance coverage from my new company kicking in.

And of course, it was not until Rene passed away and I contacted the insurance company that I found out about the error. Unfortunately, a little too late. I was going to have to figure out a way to pay all Rene's funeral expenses out of my own pocket. Let me just go to my backyard and pull a few Benjamins off the money tree I have been growing.

Exactly. On top of the grief of losing my sweetheart, I now was in an extreme financial hardship. He deserved to have an appropriate funeral, and to be honored and remembered. So I did the only I knew to do that would work. I prayed.

And of course, God answered and came through. Now, at about this point, you may be asking: Well, what about Rene's family? Couldn't they have helped? Both of

Good-bye

his parents and all his siblings except one were still living. Maybe you think I was too angry with them or too proud to ask for help in burying their son, brother, uncle, cousin, etc. No, I wasn't. I did ask, and assistance was refused. The family was coming here for the funeral, but there would be no financial assistance whatsoever extended. And that is all I will say about that topic.

In spite of the life insurance gap, in spite of the lack of support from Rene's family, God did what God always does. He made a way.

God blessed that the church I was going to helped me some financially. Someone there also suggested a funeral home that was run by another church, so funerals were its ministry, not just a business.

The funeral home was willing to accept money down and then allow me to make payments for a few months thereafter. The only outstanding thing was the plot, and for that, I had to come up with some serious money. And God made a way.

BeeCause You Loved Me

I went through the list of all the things I was getting ready for on Saturday the twentieth, the day of the funeral. Burial plot? Check. Casket? Check. Program for Rene's home going (memorial) service? Check. Eulogy written? Check. Picture for program selected? Check. Song and slide show created? Check. Trying to figure out what I was supposed to wear to my husband's funeral? Impossible!

Just what is one supposed to wear to put her husband in the ground? What is one supposed to wear to get up and speak to a crowd of people about the love of her life? How was I supposed to "dress" for my husband's funeral? God help me. Please, God, help me.

It was nine thirty Friday night and I was at Nordstrom in Bellevue, alone, trying to find an outfit to wear. I looked around but couldn't find things. Finally, an older saleswoman came up to me and said, "Can I help you find something?"

With tears in my eyes, exasperation on my face, and exhaustion in my voice, I said, "Yes. My husband died, and

Good-bye

tomorrow is his funeral, and I have to find something to wear, and I can't find anything!"

That dear, sweet woman looked at me and almost cried herself. She said, "Don't you worry, dear, we will find you something. What do you want? What size are you? I will help you find it."

And, with only twenty minutes before the store closed, she did indeed help me find something to wear. As I stood there in the dressing room looking at myself in the mirror, I realized that I was wearing "the outfit." It took everything in me not to cry. Because I knew if I did, I would not be able to stop, and I still had to drive home.

Standing in my closet that night, looking for an accessory, I turned around in circles and wondered how I was going to make it through the next day. I was exhausted. I had taken the week off from work to plan the funeral, but had worked from home every day.

It had been time to create the annual budgets for my P&Ls, and death or no death, the budget projections were due. There was a process by which each item was dependent upon another, with the ultimate goal of getting approval from the board of directors. Everything leading up to that point was based on a timeline. So, I wrote Rene's eulogy, picked out his casket, managed three different multimillion-dollar budgets, planned a funeral, and prepared for an executive training course I was going to on the following Tuesday.

All of that I had managed very well. But the funeral. It made it real. The love of my life was gone, not coming back. There would be no miraculous healing. When he died, all hope of ever returning to any resemblance of the life we all once lived as a happy family died with him.

Just at that moment, when I felt like I could not go on, God stepped in. I mean, He literally stepped in. I felt the Holy Spirit wrap itself around me like a blanket, and I got peace in my spirit, strength in my body, and calmness in my heart. The next day was Rene's Celebration of Life service. We were celebrating his life, who he was, and what he had meant to all of us. I was going to speak, and I was not just going to make it through the day. I was going

Good-bye

to enjoy remembering my love and sharing those memories with the people that love both of us.

God gave me peace and anointed me with an unbelievable amount of grace. God gave Rene and I both a beautiful gift that night as I stood in my closet, God showed me just how much He had been carrying me through the last three years, and how without Him, I never would have made it.

Not only did I make it through Rene's Celebration of Life service, but it truly was a blessing. My friends and family were there to support me. My Uncle Felix sang and his wife, Aunt Ruth Ann, played for him. I made the programs for the service and the church printed them. God had also put on my heart to do a "Rene's Life" slide show of pictures of him, his family, his boys, me and my kids, and ministry meetings and events he had done.

For the slide show, I used the only song that seemed fitting for the occasion. It was the same song we had used as our wedding's theme song: "Because You Loved Me" by Celine Dion. The lyrics, along with the pictures of Rene, told the story all by themselves. On purpose, I used only three pictures of Rene taken after the accident. I wanted everyone to remember the incredible, loving, and caring man. I wanted everyone to remember why we all loved him so much, and to understand why I fought for him so much—because he deserved nothing less than the best, no matter what condition he was in.

The song told our tale: being his strength when he was weak, being his voice when he was unable to speak, and being the person I am today because he loved me. Moreover, during those three years and one day of the nightmare we lived, I would sing that song to Rene and tell him, "Baby, as long as you fight in there, I will keep fighting for you out here." Then, I would tell him that I am the woman I am today because he loved me. What an honor and privilege it was to have such an incredible man love me so much that it healed my heart. Little did I know before this journey began, that the love Rene gave me would not only be strong enough to heal my heart, but to reinforce my heart in such a way that it has been able to

Good-bye

survive the ultimate pain: losing the very one that caused me to heal.

Although a pastor would do the eulogy, I decided that I would speak that day. Speak at my own husband's Celebration of Life service? Yes, I felt that I would be remiss if I did not. It was my one opportunity to stand before everyone—friends, family, and foes (Rene's family)—and convey my feelings and heartfelt appreciation to the very special people who stood with me through this horrible ordeal.

I thanked the people who were caregivers and took extra-special care of Rene, me, and my children. I thanked my "heart friends," who loved me so much that mere words seemed woefully inadequate to convey how deeply my soul and family had been blessed by their unending and selfless love and care. And lastly, but definitely most importantly, I thanked my family.

I have not spent enough time in this book conveying how incredibly selfless and forgiving my children were through all this. I keep asking myself, "How did I get so blessed?"

These children—with all the challenges, struggles, uncertainties, stresses, and issues that teenagers with normal family situations have to face—my wonderful children met these challenges and survived the heartbreak of knowing the only man who had truly loved them and treated them like a father should, with unbelievable grace from God.

I am truly blessed. They sacrificed, figured out their homework on their own on those nights when I had to stay overnight at the hospital, cooked, cleaned, found rides to places they needed to go, and on top of all that, took time to encourage me.

Thank you, Tyeshia and Joshua. At the writing of this book, you are nineteen and seventeen, respectively, and I see you willingly yielding to the hand of God in your lives to walk in your destiny. Tyeshia has finished her first year of college and is majoring in youth ministry and minoring in music; a wonderfully fitting course of study for her. She plays the cello, piano, and guitar, and is a gifted and

Good-bye

anointed songwriter (both lyrics and music). Combining her love, passion, and beating heart for God and youth with her musical talents seems to be exactly where God wants her, and she is walking in her destiny.

Joshua has finished his junior year of high school, and finished his first year of college at the same time through a program in the school district which allows him to go to college and get both matriculated and high school credits. By the time he graduates from high school, he will have an AA in marketing management at the age of eighteen! Also fitting, as it looks like he is going to go into music production, utilizing his incredible ear, artful and skilled playing of the alto saxophone, and remarkable business ability.

If it sounds to you like I am writing as a proud parent, it is because I am. But more than that, I am very grateful to God for keeping my children—their minds, hearts, and sanity—when all things in the natural world indicated that they should be the exact opposite of the wonderful young adults they have become.

BeeCause You Loved Me

Now you have an idea of how I thanked my children, mother, brothers, and other family members that were there for me. My mother insisted that I call her anytime, day or night, if something was going on with Rene. I cried on the phone with her, and more nights than I can remember, she and my brother Rod would show up in the wee hours at whatever hospital Rene had been rushed to, and would sit with us as we tried to figure out what was wrong with him that time.

More than my mother being physically present, she prayed and interceded for me. Called out to God for me and Rene, fasted, fell on her knees, wept, and poured her heart out to God on behalf of us. She doesn't know that I know all this, but God showed me a glimpse of her cries before His throne of grace, and her faithfulness in her petitions to Him.

As I said, mere words of appreciation and adoration were insufficient for the amount of emotion and gratitude I tried to convey.

After the service, we went to the cemetery and put the shell of Rene to rest. His brother Steve wrote a very

Good-bye

sweet and funny poem to read to him before we put the casket in the ground.

At the end of the ceremony, as we were preparing to go back to our cars, Steve stopped me, looked at me with tears in his eyes, and said, "I know why now. I thought I understood before, but now I truly know why Rene loved you so much...and I think the rest of the family is finally starting to get it."

My eyes welled up with tears, and all I could say was, "Thank you." You see, it was a very nice thing to hear, but what they thought of me did not matter anymore. It had not mattered for a long time. I determined that I was going to live my life to the best of my ability and do what I thought was best for Rene, my children, and me. I am not saying that I made all the right choices or decisions, but I can say that I made them out of love in my heart for Rene, fear for the safety of his life, and a will to try to keep some resemblance of peace in our lives. As for the rest, let God be the judge.

BeeCause You Loved Me

To end the day, my dear sweet mother had made fried chicken, potato salad, fruit salad, a green salad, Hawaiian rolls, hummingbird cake, 7Up pound cake, and much more to feed our family and my close friends that returned to my home with me.

Everyone stayed, for hours. We did not cry; we did not belabor the fact that an incredible soul that graced us with his presence on this earth for all too short a time was now gone. I did not talk about the fact that I now knew that our bed would forever be empty of his wonderful presence. I would never smell his scent on the sheets or pillow again. I would never hear him call me his "Little Thing" again. I would never feel his touch, or his warm breath on my ears, as he would reach over and say, "I love you, Little Thing. I love you."

During the fellowship at my house that night, we did not discuss the fact that never again would I hear his laugh or see the twinkle of mischievousness in his eyes as he looked at me. At no time here on this earth would he and I ever have the opportunity to play footsie under the dinner table, or make out in our cars again.

Good-bye

I did not mention that the days of us taking showers together, cooking together, working in the yard together, having pillow fights with the kids, taking long road trips to the coast, or hopping on a plane had been forever silenced by the separating of his soul from his body.

Nor did I convey the fact that the opportunity to feel his arms wrap around me and to experience an incredible feeling of safety and peace were forever and irrevocably gone.

Tyeshia and Joshua would not have the opportunity to put whipped cream on his face while he was sleeping or tickle him again. Or, for Tyeshia to hide in the closet when he came home from work, and jump out and scare the poor man who had a full bladder from commuting in rush-hour traffic. Rene and Joshua would never again go to the sporting goods store together and get "guy stuff" like weights, benches, gloves, and the like. We would never, ever again have a movie night with all four of us sitting on the couch, laughing, crying, or jumping from something seen in the movie.

BeeCause You Loved Me

We did not talk about those things at all, for those were the things that were now part of our old lives. That day was dedicated to the Rene we knew, not the Rene that was gone, so we talked about how he lived!

We talked about how he would make us laugh, how we loved his preaching and prophesying. And in the midst of it, something happened. About fifteen minutes into our multi-hour celebration of his lifetime, we began to talk loudly, laugh, make jokes, and truly enjoy each other's company. And no, there was no alcohol involved. But I will tell you what was involved. I believe that for the very last time, we had the opportunity to feel the presence of Rene's wonderful spirit and personality. It felt like Rene was there. As a matter of fact, a few times I caught myself looking around because the party felt just like the old days, when he was there. And I believe he was. Why wouldn't he have been? We were all there to celebrate his life. Rene was the guest of honor, and although absent in body, we all felt his presence.

After all was said and done, after the last person left, I realized that now it was time for me to figure out what I

Good-bye

was going to do in my life. It was time for me to figure out
how to live.

27

Live!

You probably read the title of this final chapter and thought: All right, here comes the happily ever after part. Because, of course, every great story ends with the heroine somehow having her life's dreams fulfilled, or some type of magical or divine intervention comes along and makes everything perfect, and warms the readers' hearts. Well, I hate to disappoint you, but this book is about real life and not a fairy tale. And the thing about real life is that it is as unpredictable. As unpredictable as the weather in Seattle, and does not always happen the way we think or hope it should.

Live!

But I can tell you this: I made it through what would have been Rene's forty-ninth birthday on November 6, 2007; through my first Thanksgiving, Christmas, and New Year's without Rene here on this earth; and I thought I was doing pretty well. It was amazing to me that I was experiencing "firsts" all over again. Hadn't I already gone through these three years before? Now, instead of "firsts" since his accident, it was "firsts" since his death. Talk about grieving twice! But for all intents and purposes, to my mind I was handling it all very well. That is, until February 2008.

Something began to happen in my body and with my emotions that was completely out of character for me. I began to have extreme and uncontrollable mood swings, which were very uncharacteristic for me. I was the woman about whom everyone would comment that they could not believe I had been so poised during Rene's emergencies; how I had walked in God's grace and stayed levelheaded through all this.

BeeCause You Loved Me

What I know now, but did not know then, was that my body literally had had enough of all the stress, sorrow, and grief. Suddenly, in February, I started going into what I now call "hibernation mode." Much like with a laptop computer, when you choose the option to shut it down temporarily, but keep everything just as it is, all the programs open like you left them, until you turn on the laptop again. I was fatigued all the time, beyond any form of exhaustion I had ever experienced. My body began to ache, and my mind was unclear and unfocused.

It seemed that these things got worse during the beginning of my monthly cycle, so I thought that maybe I was going through some kind of hormonal change—or, heaven forbid—premature menopause.

I had noticed this phenomenon in January some, and someone had asked if it was "that time of the month," and it was. During my cycle time in February, I became scared when I was driving down the street and talking to my best friend on the phone, and all I could do was cry. And, at that very moment, I could not think of one good reason why God still had me living here on this earth.

Live!

I did not think I would ever find true love again; I did not want to be here without Rene. I didn't want to find true love again because I knew that I would either die and put that person through the hell that I was going through, or that person would die and I would have to walk through this hell all over again. Either way, I was not seeing the bright side of things at all. Not only was I not seeing any silver lining in the clouds, I was in the darkest place I had ever been in my life. And prayer, positive thinking, talking, encouragement from friends and family; none of these were working. I could feel myself sinking into the depths of something I had no control over, and I was terrified that, like in quicksand, the more I struggled, the more I would sink.

After I returned home one evening, I was talking to my mother on the phone and telling her how despondent I was. At that point, standing in my kitchen, I realized that there was something very wrong with me medically that I could not control. That is when I called my gynecologist's office and set up an appointment to go see my doctor. I thought I had a serious hormonal imbalance.

I have to stop here and say that I love my gynecologist. He has been my doctor for almost ten years now, and he is wonderful. He is not only brilliant; he has an incredible bedside manner, a great personality, and an earnest caring for his patients.

But as I sat in the guest chair across the desk from him that day, what he was about to say to me was not what I expected to hear.

I expected him to say something like, "Monique, you have a hormonal imbalance going on and we need to adjust your estrogen level." However, what he said was, "Monique, I think that you are experiencing some Post-Traumatic Stress Disorder symptoms, and possibly grief-induced depression."

Huh? Post-Traumatic Stress Disorder (also known as PTSD)? I had not been in a war, in Iraq or Afghanistan serving in the armed forces. I had been right here in the good old US of A, living just fine. Seeing the expression on my face, he must have known what I was thinking, because he began to explain that what I had experienced with Rene had been extremely traumatic for me. I had

Live!

lived with significantly high stress for three straight years. I had not had REM sleep or dreamt in three years. I had been constantly on call for the nursing home and hospitals.

On top of all that, I was still working in an executive job, which required a minimum sixty- to eighty-hour work week; I was raising two teenagers on my own; and I was dealing with the stress of financial issues as well as trying to manage all that.

There had been too much stress on my system and my adrenal glands had been working on constant high demand for three straight years. My body was worn-out, and now that I no longer had to fight for Rene, my body could final allow itself to feel and experience all the stress I had encountered for the past three years.

I was shocked. No hormonal issue? Was he trying to tell me that I was going crazy? Because I truly felt like I was sometimes. This was so not like me. However, as he continued to talk and explain this to me, it all made sense.

My brain had been on overdrive, running at five thousand-plus RPMs, and had burned out many cylinders.

Great. Now *I* was sick. But, I realized that all was not lost. I got the medicine and counseling I needed, and I took a sabbatical from work. It was time for me to concentrate on healing myself. I had been working in my field without any kind of break for fifteen years. And, it was time for me to spend some time on myself to get healthy again, because if I did not, I was afraid that other, more permanent and detrimental things would start "crashing," and I would end up in serious health trouble.

So, I began to focus on me. Monique L. Muñoz. I did even more soul-searching, crying, reflecting, laughing about the good times, and introspection than I had done during the previous three-year journey. What you have to understand is that this type of introspection, praying, seeking God, reflecting, and growing had become a normal part of my everyday life. But this was what I would call intensive.

I slept a lot the first couple of weeks. The absence of REM sleep for three years and all the stress I had gone

Live!

through had caught up with me. My body was saying, "What? We don't have to get up and go to work? No phone calls in the middle of the night? No all-nighters in hospital emergency rooms? WORD! We are sleeping!"

So, sleep I did. And, within a couple of weeks, I began to feel better. I started feeling like the real me. No, more like a new me.

I was able to spend more time at home, cook some meals, and just enjoy life—realizing that tomorrow is not promised to any of us, so I need to enjoy what I have now.

However, there was one thing troubling me. I missed companionship. I missed being in love and having the wonderful opportunity to love someone. It is a little difficult to explain, but it had now been going on four years since I had been held, kissed, or made love to; four years since I had gone to the movies or been taken out to dinner by someone (a man) I truly cared for.

And, once you have experienced a soul mate with an unconditional love that causes your heart to expand beyond a capacity you could ever even fathom and then you tragically lose that person, it causes your heart to ache intensely to share that kind of love again.

Many have quoted Shakespeare to me, "It is better to have loved and lost, than never to have loved at all," attempting to comfort me. I say, "Bull!" The only people who quote that phrase are people who have never experienced true love. I am so emphatic about my point of view on this for one simple reason.

When you have had the opportunity to have your heart expand beyond its normal regions and then fill to its capacity, to a point of overflowing with an almost intoxicating and agape-type love, the absence of that love and the person with whom you shared it causes pain in your heart not equal to the amount of love shared. The pain is multiplied exponentially. The depth of the hole that is left is bottomless, and the aching of the heart with every beat is felt with an intensity that makes the pain of childbirth feel as if you have stubbed your toe.

This pain is what I could not process through. Then one day, I was talking to a dear friend of mine and told

Live!

him that I was having trouble moving forward, and could not understand why. My friend said to me, "It is because you are trying to live in the past. The past is a point of reference only, and not a place for you to live. You cannot drive a car forward while you are looking backward."

"Is that why I keep crashing?" I asked.

"Yes."

What a revolutionary change and paradigm shift in thinking for me. Now, at this point I would love to be able to tell you that the simple conversation and my paradigm shift catapulted me into a new reality of thinking and living. But it did not. It was one of many components of a complex puzzle that, unbeknownst to me, God was putting together to get me to a point where I would finally see the whole picture clearly.

The next "light bulb" moment came in a conversation with another friend of mine several weeks later, talking about Rene and how I was finding it difficult to accept that I had to stop loving him.

BeeCause You Loved Me

He asked, "Why do you have to stop? You will always love him. The form has changed, but your heart will always have a special place for him. No one can take away what you shared, and your love does not have to stop."

Wow. For some reason, letting go of Rene, accepting his death, to me had meant that I had to stop loving him. An incredible peace came over me when I realized that it was OK to still love him. As a matter of fact, after that discussion, I felt my heart change. It shifted from fiercely fighting to maintain its rhythm of love for Rene to accepting that a portion of it will always have the right to beat for him. No longer was my whole heart struggling to hold on to its love for Rene; it and I now understood that it was OK to cherish the love we had while still moving on with my life.

By the time some of these things had happened, and I had rested and started having a bit of fun in my life, May had come around. Time for another and probably one of the hardest "firsts" I would have to face: the first wedding anniversary since Rene had died. May 22, 2008, would have been our fourth anniversary, and it was the first one

Live!

where I would not be able to kiss and hug him, and tell him in person how much I loved him. It was the first where I would not be able to look into those big, gorgeous brown eyes of his and see him saying with them, *I love you, too, Little Thing*.

It was the FIRST. And, I found myself falling into what I referred to as my "dark place." You know that place, where the roller coaster of your emotions takes you in one direction—down—with no intention of coming up on the other side anytime soon. I felt my heart breaking, my emotions going into the abyss, and frustration at myself because I had not expected the wave to hit me the way it did.

So, I attempted to take control of the situation before it got so bad that I would decide to just stay in bed. I did two key things. One, I belonged to a particular online organization that has message boards, and although it is not a religious one, it is not uncommon to see prayer requests posted. So, I briefly described my dilemma and how my heart was breaking, and asked for prayer.

BeeCause You Loved Me

Within fifteen minutes of my post, I spiritually felt a positive difference. Regardless of what you may or may not believe, I am a walking and breathing testimony that prayer does indeed change things. I received almost a hundred posts from people supporting me in prayer, not to mention e-mails, IMs, and many phone calls from my brothers and sisters on the board supporting me. Their prayers uplifted my spirit and I felt my strength coming back.

The second thing I did was to decide that it was time for me to get away. For months, people had been telling me that I should go away by myself. However, I declined to do so, because I knew I was not ready. I knew that I would go away, spend a lot of money, and do exactly what I was doing at home—feel miserable. I knew I had not been ready to do that. It was not that I minded spending time alone; I actually have grown to enjoy the quiet time quite a bit, and have had plenty of it, with my daughter living in a dorm and my son's crazy college and extracurricular activities schedule making his time at home minimal.

Live!

Not wanting to go away alone had more to do with me not wanting to deal with going away without Rene. I had not previously wanted to go somewhere because I knew that all I would think about was the fact that Rene was not there to share the experience with me. Now, don't get me wrong; I had traveled to several places in and out of the country since Rene had passed, but for either business or ministry-related trips. This trip would be strictly and solely personal, and just for *me*!

I knew that I now was ready for the ultimate "me" time. I felt in my spirit that it was time for me to go. I only had a few more chapters of this book to write, and I knew it was time for Monique to go away for some healing and quiet time.

I knew that I needed to go to a place where I would be close to water. At first, I thought about going to the Oregon Coast; however, I did not want to make the long five-hour drive it would take to get there. But I needed water. Water helps calm, relax, and refocus me. It helps me focus on God, nature, and life, and get out of my everyday thinking patterns.

Then it hit me: Snoqualmie Falls! It is less than forty-five minutes from where I live. There is an absolutely amazing hotel there that I had stayed at before on business, and I would be able to experience the power and beauty of the falls, which were particularly stunning due to the snow cap that year.

Snoqualmie Falls it was! I called and asked for a specific room, which would allow me to walk outside directly from it, hear and see the falls, and even work outside on the small patio if I wanted to. I made the reservation for Tuesday through Friday; I would arrive two days before my anniversary, stay through the night of it, and check out the following day.

I determined that I was going to work both on "me" and on finishing this book. So, I packed my gear—laptop, a double ream of paper, printer, USB wireless mouse, cell phone, Bluetooth headset, iPod, portable speakers, candles, lavender bubble bath and lotion, spa sponge,

Live!

sweats and tennis shoes to walk in, some nice clothes to wear to dinner—loaded up my car, and hit the road!

The drive to the hotel was uneventful. No highways, freeways, or crazy traffic to deal with; just a rural two-lane road that winds around and leads to the falls. A perfect way to start my journey. And during this drive, I somehow realized that I would not return as the same person I was when I arrived. I could sense it. Little did I know how profound this journey would end up being.

This amazing hotel sits right next to the falls and provides a wonderful view of them from the restaurants as well as many of the guest rooms. Once you get to the falls, it feels like you are in another world.

I pulled up to the valet, told him my name, and gave him my keys. As he unloaded my bags and all my stuff from the car, I thought, *This is going to be great!* I was so excited; it felt incredibly wonderful to be taking some time for me.

I entered the hotel, checked in, and went to my room. It was just as expected. All the rooms have a rustic look, but when you walk in, it is into sheer elegance. Each room has a large wood-burning fireplace with hearth and is stocked with fresh wood, instant flame logs, kindling, paper, and matches.

The bathroom touted a beautiful Jacuzzi tub that was large enough to fit four people. The tub came complete with a waterfall-type faucet, programmable jet settings, and even multicolored and programmable underwater lights. The two wooden shutters could be opened to see the bedroom.

There was a king-sized bed with a beautiful comforter and more than enough pillows. The room had a desk and straight chair, two large and comfy club chairs, and my favorite part: windows that actually opened and allowed me to hear the falls and smell the wonderful air. The coup de grace was the patio with chairs to sit in and watch the falls.

What more could a writer ask for to inspire her creativity? Nothing. God had destined me to be there, at that time, and I could not wait to see what he had in store for me!

Live!

That Tuesday evening, I went to the more casual restaurant and ate dinner alone, sitting by a window and looking out at the beauty and power of the falls. People at a couple of different tables made small talk with me, but for the most part, I was left to my thoughts, and I loved it. I thought, *Why didn't I do this sooner?* And then I realized that it was because I was not ready before.

After dinner, I went back to my room, wrote a few more chapters of this book, watched some television, built a fire in the fireplace, and took a bath in the amazing Jacuzzi tub. I got out of the tub, wrapped myself in one of the big, soft, white robes, and enjoyed my solitude. I was definitely going to have to do this more often!

On Wednesday, there were two sightseeing things I wanted to make sure I did before I left. I knew I needed to see the falls, walk the trails, go to the observation deck, and spend some time praying and thinking. So, after ordering breakfast and eating in bed, I put on my sweats and tennis shoes, popped my iPod in my pocket, put in my earphones, and started walking to the beat of the music.

BeeCause You Loved Me

By the time I reached the falls—it was not a long walk from my room to the observation deck—I was already in a contemplative mood. I knew there were emotions I had to access and deal with in order to be able to finish writing some of the most difficult chapters of this book. But more importantly, I knew there were things I needed to deal with in order for me to heal. And I knew it was time for me to finish that process.

What I did not know was how God had determined he was going to get me to that point. There was a song, often played on the radio and very popular at the time, that talked about saying good-bye to a loved one. Every time I heard that song it made me cry. But I had planned for this occasion and loaded it in my iPod. Why? Not to torture myself, but because I know myself. I knew that I needed to draw forth those deep emotions and deal with them, and that the song would be the vehicle to help me arrive at that destination.

So I began to play the song, and I started praying and softly talking aloud to God and Rene, and all the emotions came rushing in. And suddenly, it was as if I could hear

Live!

Rene saying, "You promised me, Little Thing. You promised me that you would be OK. I only left because you said you would. It is time for you to be OK now."

Tears began to flow quietly down my cheeks, and as the emotions swelled inside me, I felt something like a slow release valve opening in my psyche. Then God spoke these words to my heart: "You never said good-bye to Rene."

Those two things hit me like a ton of bricks, and for a moment, I had to catch my breath. After that, I responded aloud and said, "You are right, Rene. I did promise you I would be OK. And from this day on, I will be. I gave you my word, and your Little Thing will be OK."

And then I did something I had needed to do since Rene died, but had not realized it. I audibly said good-bye to my love. It went something like this:

"Baby, I love you and will always love you. You will always have a special place in my heart, and nothing will ever change that. But I have been carrying you with me, and have not let you go. I have to let you go. I have to say good-bye, baby. In order for me to be OK, I need to let you go. You will always be a part of me. I am the person I am today, in part, because you loved me, and I am so grateful that I was blessed with the opportunity to experience your love. But it's time for me to close this chapter of my life, and see what God has in store for me. I love you, baby, and I always will, but I have to say good-bye."

With my hand over my heart and tears rolling down my face, I looked up to the heavens and bid the love of my life good-bye. I released both him and me to be free and live in the realm to which we are currently assigned: Rene in the heavens, and me here on earth.

I walked and cried for a little while after that, feeling the finality in my emotions and the release in my spirit. I could feel the void, as I had called it, in my heart tangibly shrinking. The excruciating pain of my broken heart was subsiding, and the shattered pieces were somehow reconnecting, making it whole again. And by the time I got back to the steps of the hotel, I felt like a different

Live!

woman. But there was one last thing God had in store for me.

I knew before I got to the hotel that I wanted to go into the library during my stay. I had been in there on my previous visit and loved it. I love books anyway, but this library had a large fireplace, comfortable chairs and sofas, a large, rustic chandelier, and old books. There is just something wonderful about the smells of leather, a fire, and old books. So, as I entered the hotel, I felt compelled at that moment to visit that wonderful room.

I was hoping that I would be alone in the room to continue further processing my thoughts; however, to my disappointment, there was a teenage girl sitting at the computer in it. *Oh, well*, I thought, *I have my headphones on; I can still be in my own world.* So I walked over to the wall of bookshelves and perused the books. What was interesting was that the hotel had many books that were in multiple volumes. And that was when God hit me with His final blessing and surprise of my visit.

BeeCause You Loved Me

He showed me this in a vision. I heard Him speaking ever so gently to my heart, and He said, "Just like these books, your life is made up of many volumes. You have been thinking you are closing a chapter of your life, but it is actually a volume. Your love for Rene and life with him has been written and is forever printed in this volume of your life"—He showed me a beautiful book in my mind's eye—"and you can go back and read it any time you want. You can review its contents, remember the things that occurred, and savor the memory of your love. But, it is time for you to take this volume and put it on the shelf. No more is this the current stage of your life, but rather a memory."

Then, in my mind's eye, I saw myself putting this beautiful book high up on one of the shelves and pushing it back. The next thing I saw in front of me was another book, which looked quite similar to the previous one, but was different in one way. It was open to where the spine would naturally make it part in the middle and the pages were blank.

Live!

The Lord spoke these final words to me: "This represents your new life, your new start. The pages of this volume of your life are blank and waiting to be written. It is time for you to go, live, and fill the pages of this volume."

And that, my dear friends, is exactly what I am trying to do. If you gather nothing else from this book, please love with the fullness and innocence of a child, laugh like you have lost your mind, and live like there is no tomorrow, because tomorrow is promised to no one.

I can, *Bee*Cause God allowed me to experience the depth of His love through Rene Arthur Muñoz loving *me*, and I choose to LIVE!

Life isn't about waiting for the storm to pass...it's about learning to dance in the rain.

BeeCause You Loved Me

In Loving Memory of Rene A. Muñoz

1958–2007

Love out of need always leaves one wanting more. Love out of a desire to give replenishes itself daily.

—Monique L. Muñoz

10191953R00152

Made in the USA
San Bernardino, CA
07 April 2014